TRUMP'S PATHOLOGICAL PRESIDENCY

Also by René J. Muller

The Marginal Self
Anatomy of a Splitting Borderline
Beyond Marginality
Psych ER
Doing Psychiatry Wrong
The Four Domains of Mental Illness

TRUMP'S PATHOLOGICAL PRESIDENCY

A
Malignant Narcissist
Subverts
Truth, Justice
and the
American Way

RENÉ J. MULLER, PHD

ISBN 13: 9781071115428

Cover Image: BarBus from Pixaby
Cover Design: René J. Muller
Cover Execution: René J. Muller, Diego Rosales and Amnet Systems
Interior formatted and composited by Amnet Systems
Typeset in Calibri

Dedication

To *The New York Times* opinion columnists, reporters, editors, managers and publishers

and

The Late Show host Stephen Colbert, his writers, directors and producers

for fearlessly holding Donald Trump's unreality up to a mirror so as to decode his antics, lie by lie, and for giving us hope that the miscarriage brought on by the 2016 electoral college might not, after all, hemorrhage into a second presidential term.

Acknowledgments

Martin and Carol Stacey contributed financially to the support of this project, as they have to earlier projects. Lynn Summerall followed the writing and production of the text and offered many creative suggestions about content and formatting. Tommye Allen, John Allen, Jay Allen and Claire Jones read the manuscript and identified a number of instances where an idea could be better expressed. The technicians at Vitalyst, as they have for many years, with other projects, resolved countless computer snags that temporally brought the work of writing this book to a frustrating halt. Thanks to the Kindle Direct Publishing (KDP) Customer Support Team who, though far away, responded quickly and graciously to the panicked calls of a writer inexperienced in the ways of ebook production.

Contents

Preamble

On January 12, 2017, I began to record observations, my own and those of others, about Donald Trump and his presidency, in a Word file that I named "Trump Watch." After several months, it occurred to me that I was, in fact, writing an article. As the months of Trump's presidency wore on—with his transgressions accumulating and my Word file lengthening—I began to be concerned that the text was becoming too long for an article. I was also accumulating a good many quotes, mostly from *The New York Times*, but from other sources as well. At some point, I felt the need to add references to what I realized was becoming a rather long essay.

I wish to acknowledge a considerable debt to *The New York Times*. In a country and a culture that appear to be generally in decline, the *Times* only gets better, evolving to meet the new challenges of changing times. The Trump presidency was one of these challenges, and the *Times* responded heroically. Quotes taken from their news reports and op-ed analyses—"the first draft of history"—significantly enhanced my phenomenologically and psychodynamically oriented understanding of Donald Trump, the man and the president.

Preface

I t doesn't take a crack diagnostician to spot the perversity in Donald Trump's behavior. From the start, his presidency has been fraught with the kind of conflicts more often associated with mental deviance than with politics. Journalists as well as thinkers of other stripes have given us eloquent and penetrating analyses of this president's often inexplicable actions.

Why then shouldn't mental health clinicians weigh in on the subject, even as their respective professional societies were discouraging them from doing so? While the prohibition against diagnosing political figures without an interview seems generally reasonable, the blatant pathology demonstrated by Donald Trump, over a long period of time, seems to more than justify a psychiatric diagnosis.

At some point in the course of Trump's presidency, it became clear to me that the "duty to warn," which clinicians are required to follow when patients pose credible threats to others, superseded any professional order against characterizing the underlying mental derangement of a leader whose actions put this country and the rest of the world at considerable risk. Donald Trump is not our patient, but he is our president, and, as such, he poses a far greater threat than any patient ever could.

Trump's life has been a series of habitual bad acts that collectively defy the natural order of things and affront the American sense of decency. This pattern of behavior is familiar to mental health clinicians and has been characterized as malignant narcissism. My exploration of the Trump presidential psyche is grounded in a mash-up of Adolf Meyer's psychobiology and existential psychiatry, approaches that I have shown to be compatible and complementary in *The Four Domains of Mental Illness: An Alternative to the DSM-5.*

1

Catching on to Donald J. Trump

S hortly after the 2016 general election, I wrote an op-ed for *The Baltimore Sun* titled "Can Donald Trump Change His Spots?" (Muller, 2016; Appendix A). I asked whether the strong narcissistic traits he had shown all through his adult life might be mitigated when, as president, he would have to make decisions that had more profound consequences for more people than was the case with his previous work—which included building hotels and casinos, and marketing the Trump brand. The hope (against hope) was that the aura of the Oval Office, which had induced earlier presidents to overcome their limitations and nurtured their efforts to govern during difficult times would serve to offset the worst manifestations of Trump's self-absorption.

That optimism was quickly dashed for me and for others who felt that Trump deserved a chance to show what he could do as president. What we saw instead were the worst traits of a malignant narcissist, played out now on the world stage (Appendix B). Through bitter experience, clinicians have learned that this kind of pathology almost never permanently abates (as borderline pathology sometimes does), either with time and life experience, or with intensive psychotherapy.

Despite the burgeoning evidence /that the main threat to the United States these days is its own commander in chief, the American Psychiatric Association and the/ American Psychological Association continue to discourage its members from publicly weighing in on the president's mental state, stipulating that a valid psychiatric diagnosis requires a face-to-face interview (Friedman, 2017; Lieberman, 2018). We take issue with this directive and believe that by turning a clinical eye to the totality of Trump's behavior as president we can learn more about his mental state than would be revealed in any formal diagnostic evaluation.

We also feel that the "duty to warn," which clinicians are legally held to with patients who have made credible threats against others, implicitly extends to the unprecedented situation this country faces now with Donald Trump as its president. If the "worst" were to happen, how would those who were trained and trusted to diagnose and treat mental illness, who did nothing in the face of what Trump's aberrant behavior portended, ever excuse their reticence?

Even before he was elected, there were reasons to suspect that this president's actions derived less from overzealous expressions of his alleged conservative and populist ideology than from significant pathological alterations in his mental life. Later, journalists and political satirists identified his obvious narcissistic excesses. Looking deeper into Trump's psyche, some clinicians (Lee, 2017), myself included, found malignant narcissism. Long story short, during the narrative that Trump has been creating since his inauguration, there have been countless instances when he has acted more like a mental patient than like a president.

2

Productive Narcissism, Pathological Narcissism, Malignant Narcissism

Not all narcissism is pathological. A degree of healthy narcissism that allows for the evolution of a realistic and authentic self-image is necessary if a viable self is to emerge from its psychobiological elements (Muller, 2014).

Productive Narcissism

The psychoanalyst Michael Maccoby has identified what he calls "productive narcissists," who creatively cultivate this personality style by refusing to accept the way things are, then forcefully pursuing the way they believe things should be (Maccoby, 2003; 2007). Their talents and actions dramatically change the world for the better, even as they make ripples along the way, often by offending people who are less "perfect" and not as driven as they are.

While not intrinsically pathological, these narcissists sometimes get caught in the snares of their excessive self-absorption. Maccoby's productive narcissists include Bill Clinton, J. Craig Venter, Jack Welch, Oprah Winfrey and Steve Jobs, among others. (I would add Leonard Bernstein, John McEnroe and Theodore M. Hesburgh to this pantheon.) We can only wonder if Steve Jobs was thinking of himself when he volunteered: "The people who are crazy enough to think they can change the world are the ones who do" (Isaacson, 2019). The kind of change depends on whether these people are healthy-crazy (productive narcissists) or deviant-crazy (pathological and malignant narcissists).

Pathological Narcissism

Pathological narcissism is generally understood as deriving from maladaptive, defensive responses that are made to psychic trauma experienced early in life. This pathology—narcissistic personality disorder in the *Diagnostic and Statistical Manual of Mental Disorders* (DSM-5, pp. 669-672)—is distinguished from other character pathologies by an overidentification with a self-created internal mirror (a metaphor), with content that is grandiose, expansive and often lacking in moral restraint. This image then becomes a template (another metaphor) that serves as a model for the narcissist's thought, emotion and behavior, and constitutes the core of a defensive process that is created to preserve the integrity of a seriously traumatized, fragile ego (Kohut, 1971).

Pathological narcissists, feeling small and imperiled, live through a compensatory persona that is created to be unduly bold and expansive. They greatly overestimate their innate ability and the quality of their work. They are contemptuous of the rules and laws that most people follow. They lack empathy, are unconcerned about how their actions affect others and refuse to accept blame for the damage they often inflict. Their sense of entitlement exceeds anything that could be considered normal (Maccoby, 2007).

The psychoanalyst Erich Fromm left us this brief glimpse into the heart of the pathological narcissist, which emphasizes a degree of enduring self-centeredness that is difficult to grasp:

A man calls the doctor's office and wants an appointment. The doctor says that he cannot make an appointment for that same week, and suggests a date for the following. The patient insists on his request for an early appointment, and as an explanation does not say, as one might expect, why there is such urgency, but mentions the fact that he lives only five minutes away from the doctor's office. When the doctor answers that his own time problem is not solved by the fact that it takes so little time for the patient to come to his office, the latter shows no understanding; he continues to insist that he has given a good enough reason for the doctor to give him an earlier appointment (Fromm, 2010, p. 64).

Another illuminating example of this phenomenon takes the form of a joke (Fromm, p. 66): "A writer meets a friend and talks to him a long time; he then says: 'I have talked so long about myself. Let us now talk about you. How did you like my latest book?'"[1]

Malignant Narcissism

Though not included in the DSM-5, malignant narcissism, first identified as such by Erich Fromm (2010, p. 74) and further characterized by Otto Kernberg (1970) and others (Lenzenweger et al., 2018), is a far more serious pathology than the narcissistic personality disorder parsed there. Malignant narcissists

are pathological narcissists who also show significant sociopathic or psychopathic traits. This
unique character pathology involves defenses
that underlie an enduring pattern of feeling,
thought and action that is not only contrary to
the norm but often in fierce opposition to it,
and which causes problems both for them and
for those they encounter.

These defenses are resistant to potentially
corrective life experience and to professional
intervention. Insight is either fleeting and incon-
sequential, or absent altogether. The character
pathology of the malignant narcissist is more
rigid and tightly held than that originating in
similar defenses employed by those with the
DSM-5 narcissistic personality disorder.

Productive narcissists, pathological narcissists and malignant narcissists do not always
adhere to the limits that define these categories.
Productive narcissists can—and do—exhibit
destructive traits that engulf and quash their

creativity. Those with narcissistic personality disorder will sometimes, usually under duress, resort to actions characteristic of the malignant narcissist.

3

Donald Trump's Different Existence

In contrast to the abundant information at hand about Donald Trump's deviant behavior as president—more than enough for a diagnosis of malignant narcissism—the nature of his presumed narcissistic injury, or at what age this injury and his maladaptive response to it may have occurred is not known. Frederick C. Trump often acted harshly toward his son and punished him severely for seemingly minor infractions. At age 13, he banished Donald from the family home because of his bullying behavior. Donald was sent to New York Military Academy, which emphasized discipline and respect for others. It is anyone's guess what trauma his expulsion from home and subjection to military authority might have caused this young man.

Tony Schwartz, who worked with Trump on his first book, *The Art of the Deal*, first published in 1987, spent many hours interviewing and shadowing his subject. Schwartz came to believe that "Trump's world view was profoundly and self-protectively shaped by his father," with whom his relationship was, as Trump put it, "almost businesslike":

> To survive, I concluded from our conversations, Trump felt compelled to go to war with the world. It was a binary, zero-sum choice for him: You either dominated or you submitted. You either created and exploited fear, or you succumbed to it—as he thought his older brother had [Freddie Jr., an alcoholic, died at the age of 43]. This narrow defensive outlook took hold at a very early age, and it never evolved. "When I look at myself in the first grade and I look at myself now," he told a recent biographer, "I'm

basically the same." His development ended in early childhood (Schwartz, 2017, p. 70).

This account by Schwartz of Trump's early inter-actions with his father could have shaped a nar-cissistic injury, which Trump then responded to maladaptively with early narcissistic defenses. That Trump sees himself as "the same"—emotionally and behaviorally unevolved from these childhood states, due to a possible defen-sive "freeze" in his development—is consis-tent with the often-made observations that his behavior is childish, that he is callow and that he has not acquired the moral and ethical hab-its associated with mature adults.

Psychiatrist Steve Wruble has also given a good deal of thought to the effect that Fred Trump may have had on the person Donald Trump became:

Indeed, his father's intensity left its mark on the entire family. Donald's older brother essen-tially killed himself under his father's rule. This tragedy must have played a prominent role in the formation of Donald's identity and left minimal room to rebel against his father's authority, except through competition in the realm of business success. Despite their appreciation for each other, the tension between father and son caused Donald psychological wounds that still fester (Wruble, 2017, p. 278).

Trump's narcissistic mirror, and the pattern of pathological behavior that grew from it were almost certainly reinforced by his later association with Roy Cohn, who became his advisor and mentor. Very likely a pathological narcissist himself, Cohn, Senator Joseph McCarthy's lawyer during the Army-McCarthy hearings, taught Trump to hit back with exaggerated ferocity any time he was criticized—the same advice his father had given him, advice that Trump continues to follow to this day.

Trump's altered mental life can also be viewed as his "different existence," a descriptive appellation coined by the existential psychiatrist J. H.

van den Berg to designate the deformation of being that occurs in someone who is in the grip of a serious mental illness. In our analysis, we assume an existential-phenomenological stance to psychic pathology akin to that taken by van den Berg in his book *A Different Existence* (1972).

Unlike clinicians who follow the DSM-5, we do not focus on symptoms and syndromes but instead begin with Trump's *life-story*, from which the *facts* that constitute the story are identified. A consideration of the meaning of these facts makes it possible to identify the *pathological phenomena* that constitute his different existence. A valid *diagnosis* depends on keeping faith with the etymology of this word, which derives from the Greek: to know apart, to distinguish, to discern. This amounts to identifying and characterizing a *phenomenon* (Zahavi, 2019)—what is unique to one entity and makes it different from other entities.[2]

By eliciting the *difference* between how Trump has acted and what we take to be normal behavior—to a first approximation, the absence of lasting patterns of conduct that cause significant, ongoing psychic pain and damage to oneself and others—a fuller understanding emerges of what Donald Trump has done (and may yet do) than is possible from reading the work of journalists and other analysts who have written about his presidency, incisive and illuminating as much of this commentary has been.

Chris Hayes, in a review of Michiko Kakutani's *The Death of Truth* for *The New York Times Book Review* asked: "Is it possible to say anything truly profound or new about Donald Trump at this moment in time? He is describable, almost fully, in a few short words: a misogynist, a bigot, a narcissist, a con man and a demagogue. And his behavior, like the woodpecker, feels instinctual and feral: a deeply broken man who hammers away moment to moment to repair his own brokenness, and leaving nothing but a hole" (Hayes, 2018). Our answer to Hayes' interrogative is affirmative. Trump's daily—sometimes hourly—exclamations, and the often spot-on media analysis that soon follows can be systematically interrogated to yield underlying meanings and psychological structures that enlarge our understanding of what previously seemed inexplicable.

Just three months after the inauguration, David Brooks concluded that Trump's actions so far made it look like he would not be able to do his job:

> The normal incompetent person flails and stammers and is embarrassed about it. But the true genius at incompetence like our president flails and flounders and is too incompetent to recognize his own incompetence. He mistakes his catastrophes for successes and so accelerates his pace toward oblivion . . . . Trump's greatest achievements are in the field of ignorance. Up until this period I had always thought of ignorance as a void, an absence of knowledge. But Trump's ignorance is not just an absence; it is a rich, intricate and entirely separate universe of negative information, a sort of fertile intellectual antimatter with its own gravitational pull. It's not so much that he isn't well informed;

it's that he is prodigiously learned in the sort of knowledge that doesn't accord with the facts of our current dimension (Brooks, 2017a).

Brooks is clearly on to one facet of Donald Trump's different existence. To someone who does not understand malignant narcissism, Trump may seem ignorant (literally, not knowing or lacking knowledge). In fact, it is what he *knows* that makes him *look* ignorant. His ignorance is knowledge that derives from the distortions of a pathologically distorted internal mirror. This psychic structural anomaly may also explain why his attention span is short, why his grasp of issues is shallow and why his actions are often impulsive, chaotic and contradictory.[3]

Maureen Dowd, writing a month before the 2016 election, had already implicitly grasped the pathological mental structure underlying what Brooks later saw in Trump's behavior: "In Trump's alternate universe he is always the winner. If he's not, the system is rigged, the mike is faulty, the media is biased. Narcissists see only themselves in a fun-house mirror, either larger or smaller than they really are at any given moment, so it is impossible for others to convey a true picture to them" (Dowd, 2016).

In other words, Trump's narcissism is him, and he is it. Dowd's "fun-house mirror" is the metaphorical surface that Heinz Kohut (1971) chose to explain how pathological narcissists distort everyone and everything they encounter. They are warped by the constituting power of the self as active agent as it continues to defend itself against an early trauma. This ongoing defense makes it impossible for them to connect authentically and realistically with other people, and effects all their feelings, thoughts and actions. Here is where we find the core of Trump's different existence.

As I watched Donald Trump win the Republican nomination and then the presidency, I gradually came to understand that the mirror he looks into (metaphorically speaking) is not like Narcissus' single reflected image—his own face—which he had come to value above all else, but a *series of different topographical surfaces each with a different content.* Responding to the constantly changing situations he finds himself in, Trump can access the section of his fragmented mirrored self that holds the partial image he feels he needs to identify with at any given moment. Trump's "fun-house" has, in effect, multiple mirrors. His bizarre, irrational and contradictory actions are consistent with a multifaceted, topographically varied internal mirror.

Nowhere is this fractured mirror theory more convincingly born out than when Trump suddenly decided on Dec. 18, 2018 to withdraw 2,000 U.S. troops from Syria over the unanimous protestations of his national-security team—after talking on the phone with Turkish president Recep Tayyip Erdogan. The next day, Secretary of Defense James Mattis came to the Oval Office with a letter of resignation, imploring Trump to reconsider this move. Trump refused and Mattis resigned.

A few days after the Mattis firing, Bret Stephens suggested that "the problem with Trump isn't that he's an empty vessel. It's that he's a malig- nant one" (Stephens, 2018). It's not that Trump is just a nationalist, or an isolationist, or that he believes in "America First." Other American poli- ticians have had these mindsets and not dam- aged our country as Trump has done. What Stephens sees as "malignant" in Trump is a ver- sion of pathological narcissism that coexists with sociopathy and has been given the name malig- nant narcissism—with the added provision that his internal mirror is multi-faceted in a way that does not allow for considered, consensual and integrated feeling, thought or action. Trump has repeatedly exhibited a set of behaviors which constitute a phenomenon that has been desig- nated as a mental illness.

Pulling out of Syria must have delighted Russia and Iran, who have interests of their own in this country. The Kurds, our longtime allies in fighting ISIS, felt abandoned and betrayed, an action justified by Trump's lie that the U.S. had achieved its goals in Syria by having defeated ISIS.

We will probably never entirely understand why Trump's impulsive will settled on the notion of withdrawing our troops from Syria. In the phone conversation with Erdagon, the Turkish president very likely said something about our presence in Syria that either flattered or threatened Trump and he impulsively acted to either align himself with the flattery or against the threat, or possibly both. Of course, what he did, as he always does, was mostly about *him*.

The model of the multi-faceted internal mirror helps us to see how Trump's debasement of truth, consisting of alternative facts and fake news, comes so easily to him, along with his impulsiveness that is based on these shifting images. For Trump there is what he calls fake news—*The New York Times*, *The Washington Post*, *The New Yorker*, ABC, NBC and CBS news, etc.—and Fox News, the right-wing network that backed his 2016 presidential campaign.

In a *New Yorker* article titled "Trump TV," Jane Mayer (2019), the magazine's chief Washington correspondent, makes the case for a Trump-Fox

News symbiosis, where mutual needs are being met deceitfully, and at times pathologically. She quotes Matt Gertz, senior fellow at Media Matters for America: "The President's world is being specifically shaped by what he sees on Fox News, but Fox's goals are ratings and money, which they get by maximizing rage. It's not a message that is going to serve the rest of the country." A quote from Jerry Taylor, co-founder of the Washington Niskanen Center, closes out Mayer's article: "[Trump] has something no other President in American history has ever had at his disposal—a servile propaganda operation."

On those days when he is at the White House, Trump's official work schedule usually starts at 11 a.m. Rising early, often before dawn, he tweets and watches Fox News. Later in the day, and into the night, he continues to follow unfolding events and commentary on Fox, and often has phone conversations with selected members of the Fox team—those who uncritically toe the White House line. What Trump continuously sees and hears on Fox has become, for him, *the truth*, an unending series of images he internalizes that creates *his reality*, fusing Fox's external TV mirror with his own internal mirror. To a large extent, Fox is Trump, and Trump is Fox.

4

Trump Exemplifies the Malignant Narcissist

As president, Donald Trump has become an exemplar of a pathological phenomenon long known as malignant narcissism (Muller, 2018, p. 132).[4] He has put on a virtual clinic of this pathology which, unlike the behavior exhibited by those having borderline, schizoid, histrionic, paranoid and obsessive-compulsive personality disorders, can produce a creative result. Until, that is, what is pathological about the narcissist's creation inevitably engulfs what was initially seen as positive and useful, often leaving everyone involved worse off.

It is no wonder that a good deal of what Donald Trump does makes no sense to everyday perception. The image he incessantly projects of himself as a peerless dealmaker and negotiator is countered by the fact that many of his real estate deals have gone seriously sideways. Despite these fiascos, Trump's narcissistic defenses allow him to act as if he were the smartest guy in the room, the one who can outwit and defeat anyone else. He gives every indication of believing that he will survive the investigation of special counsel Robert S. Mueller III into his alleged collusion with the Russians over their interference with the 2016 presidential election, and other transgressions—because he has survived the consequences of so many prior dishonorable acts, in his personal life, in business and in politics.

Convinced of his specialness, Trump sees himself as untouchable. Just before the 2016 election, as Trump was consolidating his base, he said he could "stand in the middle of Fifth Avenue and shoot somebody and wouldn't lose any votes." In a "Fox and Friends" interview on Aug. 23, 2018, shortly after Michael E. Cohen's guilty plea and Paul Manafort's conviction, he told Ashley Earhardt, "I've always had controversy in my life, and I've always succeeded. I've always won. I've always won."

By January 2018, the Mueller investigation was seriously encroaching the White House. Trump's lawyers sent a 20-page letter to Mueller claiming that the special counsel and his committee lacked the authority to investigate their client and that even if Trump were indicted, he could pardon himself. By early June, several of Trump's former colleagues had already been indicted, and Mueller was pressuring Trump to submit to the committee's questioning. Trump's tweeted response included the assertion "[I have] the absolute right to PARDON myself."

Because Trump is Trump, he believes that he is above the law and should be the sole decider of his karma. At the same time, he sees sufficiently beyond the shell of his fictional specialness to hold everyone else strictly accountable for what *they* do, or fail to do, often recommending punishment for those who disappoint him. Not one to let bygones be bygones, he has repeatedly pilloried Hillary Clinton for her pre-election email indiscretions. At rallies, and elsewhere he has directed the cloying refrains "Crooked Hillary" and "Lock Her Up." He has often rebuked China for stealing American technology (for once, he was right). As Trump strictly holds everyone else to the rules, he gives himself an all-inclusive pass.

Trump has notoriously thin skin. When censured, his most common response is to reflexively strike back at his challengers with insults, displacing the blame onto them. Trump lives in a self-absorbed, self-referential cocoon and does not engage in an authentic dialectic with others and the world. Cut off in this way, he blocks the chance to acknowledge and learn from his mistakes. Convinced that he is always right, he feels he has no *need* to change. Trump processes most of what he experiences—including criticism—with the habitual, mal-adaptive responses that collectively shape his different existence.

5

Trump-truth: A President's Assault on Truth

Donald Trump's entitlement permits him to disregard what it means to be truthful in the conventional sense of the word. He habitually spurns the late Senator Daniel Patrick Moynihan's often-cited decree that we are entitled to our own opinions, but not to our own facts. His contempt for consensual truth and his pathological lying derive from a certainty that he *does* have the right to his own "alternative facts," and to his own version of reality based on these facts. This insistence is a hallmark of Trump's different existence, casting him as an outlier among men. Time and again, he makes it clear that he is entitled to anything he wants.

Trump-truth appears to be whatever Trump feels the "truth" needs to be at any given moment, as he deals with the issues confronting him. Requirements for this kind of truth vary with the everchanging nature of his ongoing projects and the pushback he encounters along the way. A stellar example of the malleability of Trump-truth was the sudden about-face Trump did on his first Attorney General Jeff Sessions' "zero tolerance" order to take away the children of illegal asylum-seekers. Both Democrats and Republicans condemned this action. First Lady Melania Trump and daughter Ivanka Trump urged him to reconsider. Reluctantly and resentfully, Trump did a one-eighty, while insisting that the original abduction order had come from the Democrats (a total lie) and that only they could override it.

Trump takes Heraclitus' intuition that life as we know it is always in flux—"You cannot step into the same river twice"—to a pathological degree, which is to say substantially further than anyone without his psychic pathology would take it. Lance Morrow captures the gist of Trump-truth: "[Trump's] idea of truth or falsehood is utilitarian: Absolutely everything that he does, or thinks is a negotiation with the possibilities as he sees them at a given moment" (Morrow, 2018).

If you lie often enough, as Trump does—he is a habitual liar—eventually no one will expect you to tell the truth. In repeatedly accusing everyone who disagrees with him of being a liar, he has blurred the distinction between what is true and what is false. Tossing truth aside, and more importantly undermining the importance of truth itself, Trump debases thought, reason and speech. He has worn down the critical awareness of many who still support him, convincing them that everyone is at least somewhat crooked, and that he, being the most crooked of all, is most qualified to lead the pack.

Emily Ogden has explored how this frightening ploy works: "When no one is trustworthy, you might as well trust a con-artist. There's a strange logic to the idea. Innocent lambs may be admirable, but they're not the defenders you want in a dog-eat-dog world. Better to have a sly fox at your side" (Ogden, 2018). One, that is, who isn't constrained by rules that limit the other foxes.

Frank Bruni has identified the essence of the "edge over everybody" that Trump appears to have, his "gift": "He can do no wrong because he's *all* wrong. He never really shocks because he's a perpetual shock. When someone frolics at the nadir for as long as he has, there's nowhere to go but sideways . . . . The sheer volume of his offenses, not to mention the velocity with which one follows another, renders each of them less potent, not more" (Bruni, 2018). With varying degrees of self-awareness and outright denial, those who voted for Trump and continue to support him have ultimately opted for a kakistocracy, an awful sounding, Greek derived word that means being governed by the worst people.

Sigmund Freud would have interpreted the appalling lack of character underlying Trump's behavior as the upshot of an id overtaking an ego, after silencing a superego. David Brooks has captured some of the dark currents that constitute this brand of psychic pathology:

Trump is a cultural revolutionary, not a policy revolutionary. He operates and is subtly changing America at a much deeper level. He's operating at the level of dominance and submission, at the level of the person where fear stalks and contempt emerges.

He's redefining what you can say and how a leader can act. He's reasserting an old version of what sort of masculinity deserves to be followed and obeyed. In Freudian terms, he's operating on the level of the id. In Thomistic terms, he is instigating a degradation of America's soul.

We are all subtlety corrupted while this guy is our leader. And throughout this campaign [leading up to the 2020 election] he will make himself and his values the center of conversation. Every day he will stage a little drama that is meant to redefine who we are, what values we lift up and who we hate (Brooks, 2019).

Trump's lack of a conscience and his almost total disregard for truth, law and the Constitution make him a sociopath. Functioning as all-id, monstrously self-centered and totally self-absorbed, Trump cannot imagine that anyone else is *not* as amoral and sociopathic as he is. The call to serve his country is dwarfed by a constant need to service the ever-changing demands of a pathologically inclined self. John Dowd, formerly one of his personal lawyers, concluded that if Trump were to meet with Robert Mueller, to testify before the Special Committee, as he was being pressured to do, Trump would inevitably commit perjury—by force of habit.

The Big Enough Lie

We all know the old saw that if you tell a big enough lie, people will believe it. The source of this insight, steeped in depravity, is Adolf Hitler, and appears in his *Mein Kampf,* an apologia, written while he was imprisoned in Germany, outlining his political ideas and plans for Germany's future. The book was published in two volumes, in 1925 and 1926:

[I]n the big lie there is always a certain force of credibility; because the broad masses of a nation are always more easily corrupted in the deeper strata of their emotional nature than consciously or voluntarily; and thus in the primitive simplicity of their minds they more readily fall victims to the big lie than the small lie, since they themselves often tell small lies in little matters but would be ashamed to resort to large-scale falsehoods. It would never come into their heads to fabricate colossal untruths, and they would not believe that others could have the impudence to distort the truth so infamously. Even though the facts which prove this to be so may be brought clearly to their minds, they will still doubt and waver and will continue to thin' that there may be some other explanation.

the grossly impudent lie always leaves traces behind it, even after it has been nailed down, a fact which is known to all expert liars in this world and to all who conspire together in the art of lying (Hitler, 2011, p. 148) (emphasis added).

And here we have it, from one of the most self-deluded dissemblers and destroyers of life and real estate of any time—Adolf Hitler's own deep-structure analysis of the big lie. *New York Times* columnist Charles M. Blow spotted the link to Trump-truth:

[No] person of sound reason or even cursory political awareness can read this [Hitler's discourse on the big lie] and not be immediately struck by how similar this strategy of lying is to Donald Trump's seeming strategy of lying: Tell a bigger lie than people think a lie can be, thereby forcing their brains to seek truth in it, or vest some faith in it, even after no proof can be found (Blow, 2017).

Blow sees how Trump has found a way to make people believe that his lies do not come from him but "pass through him," not as a "producer" but as a "projector," often of what others have said about a topic he happens to be pontificating on. With the narcissist Donald Trump, there is no authentic *him*, just reflections projected from, and pinging around a set of pathologically fragmented internal mirrors, created long ago as a defense. All is reflection here (rather than authentic ownership) in what Maureen Dowd (2016) called the "fun-house mirror."

Trump *wills* his version of truth into being, as we all create our own valuations of and responses to what we experience. The difference is that Trump-truth is continuously created through *pathological* responses. How could an authentic self possibly flow from the Trumpian narcissistic defensive structure that is identified and characterized here? For Trump to participate in what we call consensual truth would require him to break long-standing, psychobiologically

imprinted maladaptive habits, something narcissists of all stripes strenuously resist, as any clinician who has ever worked with these patients
will attest.

Trump is no Adolf Hitler, but the parallels
between his distortion of truth and Hitler's distortions are striking. Both used lies to acquire
power and hold on to power as leaders of their
respective nations. We have seen Trump use the
"big lie" tactic time and again, during the presidential campaign and during his presidency.
Here are a few of his most outlandish misrepre-
sentations: in the 2016 election, he would have
won the popular vote as well had it not been
for widespread voter fraud; Barack Obama was
not born in the United States and was not eli-
gible to run for president; Senator Ted Cruz's
father was complicit in the assassination of JFK;
George Soros bankrolled the Honduran caravan
that was travelling toward the U.S. border at
the time; other presidents did not contact the
families of fallen soldiers to offer the thanks of
a grateful nation.

"Fake News" and Trump's Assault on Truth

Constantly calling the media's reports of his blatant lies "fake news" is Trump's biggest—and potentially most perilous—lie yet, because this one seriously threatens the very existence of the country's most independent watchdog of truth, a free press. Freudian psychoanalysts would call the big lie a "projection," a defense created to diminish the anxiety attached to certain feelings or actions by attributing them to someone else. Accuse *me* of lying? No. *You're* the liar. This dynamic is a significant component of Trump-truth. Paraphrasing Blow (2017), Trump weaponizes untruth, using the lie to assault and subdue.

To seek accomodation in a world that is often anything but obliging, we tend to blur the line between truth and however else we are conceiving its useful antithesis at the moment. We are all subject to self-deception (Fingarette, 1969), the lie we tell ourselves before we tell it, in one guise or another to someone else— often to survive (or at least that's what we tell ourselves). But Trump takes this dimensional inclination to the point where his Trump-truth *numbs* us to the truth, as Charles Blow has adroitly noted: "[Trump] wants to so blur the line between truth and lies that he's exhausted our stamina for discernment" (Blow, 2019b).

Counterpunching Trump's continuing assault on truth, *The New York Times*, from the start of his presidency, ran excoriating op-eds by Charles M. Blow, David Brooks, Frank Bruni, Gail Collins, Maureen Dowd, Paul Krugman, David Leonhardt, Emily Ogden, Bret Stephens and others (Blow, Brooks, Bruni, Dowd, Leonhardt, Ogden and Stephens are quoted here). The *Times* has also periodically printed full-page poster ads, sometimes with just a few lines of text, asserting the possibility of knowing truth, and the necessity of embracing it.

Like so many other manifestations of Trump's narcissistic pathology, his disregard for truth is related to a significant distortion of what existential philosophers, psychologists and psychiatrists call *lived time*. In contrast to the more familiar and quantitative *clock time*, lived time is the experiential way we feel and see the *now* (present) in relation to the *no longer* (past) and the *not yet* (future). The present is the point of orientation that allows us to recall what has come before, and the consequences that will follow whatever we do. Trump's creation of an ongoing, encapsulated narcissistic present, disconnected from the past or future, is a major structural flaw in his different existence. Identifying this deficit helps us to understand how he is routinely able to bypass truth in favor of other, more immediate and expedient ends, without comprehending that his indifference to the past and future is aberrant.

Trump-truth puts us in mind of George Orwell's *1984*. Probably not incidentally, sales of this dystopian novel surged in January 2017 shortly after press secretary Sean Spicer introduced Americans to the notion of "alternative facts," following the Trump camp's gross overestimation of the number of people who attended his inauguration.

6

Trump Lies, or Trump Bullshit?

In an essay for the blog *Lawfare*, written two weeks after Trump was elected president, Quinta Jurecic questioned whether Trump would be capable of fulfilling the Oath of Office that he was scheduled to take on Jan. 20, 2017. The problem: Trump believed that the Constitution and the laws derived from it do not matter. Jurecic's argument was not new, but it did include a new wrinkle—the distinction that Harry G. Frankfurt had made between lies and, yes, bullshit, in *On Bullshit*, an essay published by Princeton University Press (Frankfurt, 2005):

Frankfurt's essay is relevant not because Donald Trump is a liar, though he does appear to be one. It's important to our present moment because of the distinction the essay draws between lying, an act undertaken intentionally to obscure the truth and therefore must be performed with a knowledge of the facts, and bullshitting, an act undertaken without any relation to the truth whatsoever (Jurecic, 2016).

The liar, who knows the truth but decides to distort it for personal gain (Michael Cohen), can, with the right inducements (a shorter prison sentence) be brought around to acknowledge both the lie and the truth that was undermined by the lie. The bullshitter, on the other hand, sees no objective truth to acknowledge. Who has ever heard Donald Trump admit to one of *his* lies, even as he attacks the "fake news" aimed at outing these deceits?

Jurecic asks, "[W]hat does it mean to have a bullshit artist swear the Oath of Office and promise to 'faithfully execute the Office of

President of the United States,' when the notion of hewing 'faithfully' to any commitment is so fundamentally antithetical to the character of bullshit?" Framed as this paradoxical question, the implications of the falseness of Trump-truth seem even broader and more harrowing.

What Jurecic calls a bullshitter's "cheerful indifference to the truth" affects his sense of what the world is. "This isn't only a rejection of the concept of truth generally," she says, "but also a rejection of our ability to speak intelligently to one another on the basis of a mutual understanding of the world." Clearly, Trump's bullshit has paralyzed a government and divided a country.

Whether one chooses to call Trump's distortion of truth bullshit—or not—it seems obvious that *denying the existence* of truth, as he does, is a greater pathological perturbation of the self as active agent than merely *upending* truth, as ordinary liars do. His disregard for truth originates in and flows from the malignant narcissistic defenses identified and character-ized here, which show no sign of attenuating in response to the increasing pressure brought by those who adhere to consensual reality and the rule of law. Tuned inwardly, these isolating defenses significantly distort Trump's interac-tion with the world outside him.

One can question the ultimate validity of the liar-bullshitter distinction, but if defining "bullshit" as Frankfurt does allows us to see Trump's narcissistic pathology in sharper focus, as I believe it does, then it seems worth keeping. Perhaps bullshit is best understood as a differ-ent kind of lie, from a different kind of liar: one whose defenses are designed to make "truth" be what it needs to be at any moment so as to diminish the anxiety of participating in a world which, without these psychic dodges, would feel intolerably dangerous and unlivable.

7

Malignant Narcissism and Trump's Foreign Policy

Only someone who was completely taken with himself and intent on disregarding diplomatic precedent and history, would have blown up his participation in the G-7 summit in La Malbaie, Quebec (June 8-9, 2018) the way Donald Trump did. After trashing and alienating our closest NATO allies, he flew to Singapore to glad-hand the North Korean dictator Kim Jong Un, a longtime sworn enemy of the United States. Kim signed a document making vague promises to "denuclearize" his country in exchange for, among other things, Trump's promise to cancel the longstanding twice-yearly military exercises with South Korea, which had become a pillar of our alliance with that country. This move blind-sided South Korea, the Pentagon and just about everyone else.

Trump appears to have more in common with Kim Jong Un—he brags about their "very special bond"—and Vladimir Putin than he does with the G-7 NATO leaders. His common denominator with both men? All three are sociopaths, and, almost certainly, all three are malignant narcissists. Can we doubt that we elected a president who is less suited to lead the world's foremost democracy than he is to rule a third-world country?

Trump's attacks on our allies are ultimately attempts to take down institutions that were created from the liberal international order—the face of supportive mutuality America has shown its allies since the end of World War II—including, besides the G-7 and NATO, the European Union and the World Trade Organization. Trump is driven by an ideological hatred of any organization that promotes reciprocity among nations at the expense of U.S. world hegemony, or his own power. His campaign for domination is lubricated by a destructive nihilism, a component of his different existence.

On July 13, 2018 the Justice Department indicted 12 Russian nationals as part of special counsel Robert Mueller's investigation of Russian interference in the 2016 presidential election. Three days later, at a press conference following the Helsinki summit meeting with Vladimir Putin, Donald Trump declared: "I have great confidence in my intelligence people, but I will tell you that President Putin was extremely strong and powerful in his denial today." Impressed more by Putin's imagined "strength" and "power" than by the judgment of the grand jury and his own closest advisors, Trump sided with Russia, again calling the investigation that led to the indictments a "rigged witch hunt."

To many observers, this development was a watershed moment in the bizarre trajectory that has been the Trump presidency. The blowback was instantaneous and harsh, even from Trump's Republican supporters. Former House speaker Newt Gingrich said the capitulation to Putin was "the most serious mistake of [Trump's] presidency." Senator John McCain responded, "No prior president has ever abased himself more abjectly before a tyrant." Senator Paul Ryan acknowledged, "There is no question that Russia interfered with our election and continues attempts to undermine democracy here and around the world." Senator Rand Paul wondered if Trump's response was another product of "Trump Derangement Syndrome."

Any formal psychiatric diagnosis requires a clinician to assess how much (or little) insight patients have into their different existence, as well as the toll such an anomalous life may be taking on them and others. After observing Trump's presidency in its natural state (*in vivo*) since January 2017, how can anyone fail to see that this man does not fret over the ethical and moral dimensions of his behavior? To him, whatever he does is fine because *he* is doing it.

He finds it incomprehensible that anyone would see things differently. Trump is the sun in his own self-created solar system, with the circling planets (everyone and everything else) under his gravitational pull. His lack of self-knowledge, along with his obvious sociopathy make the diagnosis of malignant narcissism an obvious call. This narcissist's ultimate dream would be to fold America into himself.

8

Other Trump Pathologies: Secret Schizoid; Nihilist and Anarchist; Crypto Fascist; Paranoid

B esides being an exemplar of the phenomenon of malignant narcissism—roughly, the coexistence of pathological narcissism and sociopathy—Donald Trump evinces other pathological behaviors.

Secret Schizoid

Though Trump's emotional detachment is consistent with malignant narcissism, his tone-deafness and cluelessness are also characteristic of the "secret schizoid," a pathological condition identified by the psychoanalyst Ralph Klein (Masterson & Klein, 1995, pp. 25-27). Those with this indisposition assume the outward form of sociality, as Trump does so well, but otherwise have abnormal interactions with others.

As noted in *The Four Domains of Mental Illness: An Alternative to the DSM-5*, secret schizoids are "emotionally shut down and emotionally unavailable, keeping their real feelings and personalities under wrap, risking little or nothing of their inner selves as they deal with the world through a persona" (Muller, 2018, p. 156). It has been frequently noted that Trump has no close friends, only flatterers and enablers, who are quickly dismissed once they waiver in their obeisance, and that his contacts with others are strictly transactional, entailing business only. His efforts to simulate positive feelings for others in public appearances, especially with Vladimir Putin and Kim Jon Un, have been cringeworthy.

Nihilist and Anarchist

Streaks of nihilism and anarchy run through this president's malignant narcissism. Trump rejects all authority and believes that American government is corrupt and inept and should be ignored, downsized and subverted. Recognizing this mindset, we can understand why so many of Trump's actions lead to chaos, rather than to resolution and stability. With no psychic center of his own, he tends to decenter everyone and everything he takes on.

Trump's shifting narratives, particularly his incomprehensible about-faces on significant issues, create a discordance that is his favored milieu, allowing him to avoid the actual substance of an issue in play, for which he has obvious contempt and often little understanding.

Trump lies by annihilating consensual truth, and this nullification is perhaps his most encompassing nihilistic act. The real "art" of a Trump deal includes these (mostly) nihilistic elements: Throw a verbal grenade into an issue, proposal, accusation, etc.; go into attack mode, gaining the upper hand; while everyone else is still stunned and off balance, walk back some of the most contemptable elements of the attack; manipulate the participants into settling for something less awful than what was initially demanded; take sole credit for the "good" outcome.

According to many sources, Trump had always rolled this way. It was the script he followed at the end of May 2019 when he loudly threatened to impose immediate and progressive tariffs on Mexico if that country did not find a way to limit the number of refugees from Latin America crossing its border into the United States. It was widely recognized that these tariffs—5% to start, with increases if Mexico continued to demure—would raise prices for many basic products, causing great personal hardship for American buyers (Baker, 2019).

In fact, negotiations with Mexico had been progressing for months before Trump made his threat. On June 7, with the deadline he imposed fast approaching, he unilaterally announced that a satisfactory agreement had been reached, taking full credit for this "success." In fact, Trump had really backed off his threat. Many reports tagged him for exaggerating the role he played in this supposed victory. His response? "Fake news."

Michelle Goldberg saw it this way:

> Once again, Trump made a series of unhinged threats against another country, leading to high-stakes diplomacy, and the announcement of a breakthrough. One again, chest-beating conservatives jeered at Democrats for refusing to concede that Trump's belligerence had borne fruit. Once again, when the details were revealed, it became obvious that Trump had accomplished very little of any substance. And once again, Trump has created a situation where it's hazardous for his opponents to say too much about his incompetence (Goldberg, 2019b).

If the self as active agent can freely create being, this freedom must include the capacity to nihilate (at least partially) some aspects of that being as well. We all use denial as a defense to avoid what we do not want to face. This kind of self-deception is universal and is employed dimensionally, to different degrees and with different outcomes, by those who are essentially well, and by those who are neurotic and psychotic. Trump's behavior is about as far to the right in this spectrum as one can go without being overtly psychotic. He undoes, cancels, nullifies, negates, quashes, rescinds, revokes, scuttles, etc. whatever does not fit the template of the thinking, feeling and acting that has come about through his narcissistic defenses.

While operating in a present that is unbound by the past or concerned about the future, Trump eradicates from his consciousness facts that can be proven to be true—by *willing them out of his existence*. To create Trump-truth, he must annihilate *the* truth. Recalling Harry Frankfurt's and Quinta Jurecic's proposal that bullshitters have no concept of consensual truth, Trump's nihilism orients him more toward bullshit than toward straight-up lies, though some will prefer to see him as a liar.

Crypto Fascist

Donald Trump is also a crypto fascist, crypto because he hides his fascistic acts behind the mask of a bogus nationalism. He cries "America First" and "Make America Great Again," but these epithets are really cons aimed at manipulating certain minorities within our borders and rebuking other nations. He parades America's military might while disparaging its rule of law and the mechanics of an elected government, undermining the democratic way. He indiscriminately trashes political opponents and those who challenge him in the media, undercutting a free and independent press. He uses rallies to fire up crowds, toying with the feelings of those who cheer him on, while insinuating that their anger justifies violence. At times, during these gatherings, we hear echoes of Adolf Hitler. A specter of fascism haunts the Trump presidency.

Paranoid

Trump's thin-skinned paranoia, which frequently flares, is often a tactic to position himself as a victim so he can justify acting out his own aggression, often by being destructive. This defense is primarily a consequence of a deep-seated inability to trust *anyone*, what Erik Erikson in *Childhood and Society* called *basic mistrust* and R. D. Laing in *The Divided Self* called *ontological insecurity*. There can be little doubt that Trump developed this global maladaptive response to the world while under his father's thumb as a child, adolescent and adult. Fred Trump trusted no one, and taught Donald that, in any interaction with another person, one either "killed" or "was killed." The adage "The best defense is a good offense" is usually applied to sports, board games and military engagement, but holds true as well for pathological defenses employed by the human psyche. Trump learned to see life as a series of battles, and paranoia became one of his principal warring tactics.

9

Trujmp Is Not Psychotic or Demented

N o inventory of Donald Trump's malignant narcissism and related mental deviances—in toto, his different existence—would be adequate without addressing the frequently heard accusation that he is psychotic.

Psychosis

Trump often ignores and distorts reality, but he does so within the boundaries of cause and effect, even as he pushes these boundaries further than any president in memory. He constantly creates reality-busting, culture-ripping fantasies that appeal to the needs and hopes of many Americans. David Brooks has captured this phenomenon: "Trump's supporters follow him because he gets his facts wrong, but he gets his myths right. He tells the morality tale that works for them" (Brooks, 2017b). Trump tells lies that people *want* to believe.

Here's Donald Trump on the subject, in his own words, as recorded in *Trump: The Art of the Deal* (Trump & Schwartz, 2015, p. 58), the revised version of the 1987 *The Art of the Deal*:

The final key to the way I promote is bravado. I play to people's fantasies. People may not always think big themselves, but they can still get very excited by those who do. That's why a little hyperbole never hurts. People want to believe that something is the biggest and the greatest and the most spectacular. I call it truthful hyperbole. It's an innocent form of exaggeration—and a very effective form of promotion.

Trump's "truthful hyperbole" is rooted in consensual reality, and has meaning, purpose and a self-aggrandizing endpoint for its creator. Insight here is intact, except, of course, for the self-deception that allows Trump to believe his expansiveness is truthful and innocent. What Donald Trump insists is "truthful hyperbole," most people would see as a destructive lie.

The designation of psychosis is reserved for those who create lives that are significantly more removed from the instrumental world of cause and effect than the reality-based fantasy world that Donald Trump conjures. Trump is often accused of being "delusional." But his distortion of reality is less a *break* (or even a partial break) with the world of consensus, as happens in psychosis, than it is a deliberate, self-deceiving refusal to accept selected aspects of consensual reality. This rebuff is facilitated by the expansive, grandiose and entitled elements of his malignant narcissistic character pathology and by his chosen course as a demagogue.

Dementia

The claim that Trump is demented must also be challenged. In fact, none of Trump's lumpen behavior rises to the level seen in biologically driven dementing conditions. The shallowness that he so often displays is consistent with the observation made by clinicians that many pathological narcissists are "headline readers," who are loath to plumb the depths of any issue. Concerned exclusively about themselves, they would not be expected to respond to the authentic invitation of the world. Trump's chosen way to communicate—via tweet—is a lightweight's response to hefty issues where, in effect, he *writes* headlines, which are mostly false and indefensible.

Trump's capacity to grasp and resolve complex issues is limited. These shortfalls are more likely manifestations of an impaired cognition related to his malignant narcissism than the upshot of a biologically based decline in mental function, as some have claimed. The media have called him out for not "understanding" how time zones work after he repeatedly insisted on telephoning leaders of countries, on different continents at times when they were most likely sleeping. A plausible dynamic explanation for this behavior is that Trump feels entitled to call anyone he wants, for whatever reason, anytime he wants. Why should time-zone limits apply to him? Resentful of any restrictions, he cannot fathom why anyone would not be ready and willing to talk to him at any hour.

Even as Trump blusters on about his high IQ, it is possible that some of his obvious cognitive dysfunction derives from a less than scintillating mind. Unlike the *in vivo* diagnosis of Trump's malignant narcissism made here—ultimately a formal statement of the self-created, ongoing defensive stance he takes against the world— a determination of dementia—an autonomous brain disease—would require a hands-on neurological workup and brain imaging. That said, the convergence of middling IQ and malignant narcissism could go a long way toward accounting for the outright dumbness that appears to crimp so much of what Trump says and does.

Several months after making the case here that Donald Trump's behavior is not best explained as the productions of a demented brain, an incident occurred that needs to be noted. On April 2, 2019, Trump was in the Oval Office meeting with NATO Secretary General Jens Stoltenberg, with the press present. At some point, Trump urged the reporters to investigate how the special counsel Robert Mueller's investigation began. "I hope they now go and take a look at the oranges of the investigation," Trump told reporters. "The beginnings of that investigation . . . where it started, who started it . . . the Mueller report I wish covered the oranges of how it started. The beginnings of the investigation" (Serota, 2019).

These words go far beyond the Trump ramblings that we have become used to. The repeated substitution of "oranges" for "origins" is something new in this man's public productions, the kind of malapropism that is often heard from those with dementia. Though the meanings of this astonishing cognitive slippage are not evident, I would not be in a hurry to ascribe its origin to dementia.

10

Will Trump Survive His Transgressions?

In Ernest Hemingway's *The Sun Also Rises*, one minor character asks another, "How did you go bankrupt?" The answer: "Two ways. Gradually then suddenly" (Hemingway, 2006, p. 141). It is the phenomenon of "gradually then suddenly" that interests us here. Human ends are rarely achieved through strictly linear processes. This tale of one person going broke points to a universal truth: the initially slow, then accelerated rate at which this, and many other bad outcomes occur.

Some people spend more than they can afford to spend, burning through reserves, often deceiving themselves about how long their leveraging can continue. Then the axe falls, and, with this discontinuity, all chance of maintaining the illusion that solvency will be restored.

As far as we know, Donald Trump is not currently facing bankruptcy, though he has been there several times before and could eventually find himself there again. But what he *is* facing now is a comeuppance of a lifetime lived largely outside the ethical guidelines and laws that most people who do the kind of work he does observe, at least to some degree. Citizens who voted him in, and officials who were elected or appointed to make and enforce the laws of the land, are closing in on him, at an increasing rate. The "gradually" made charges that he has faced for several decades have "suddenly" grown teeth.

Two-thousand nineteen began ominously for the president. On Dec. 22, 2018 he had ordered a partial shutdown of the government after Congress refused to approve a $5.7 billion bill to fund his Mexican border wall. On January 25, 2019, after unsuccessful efforts to persuade House members, then mostly Democrats, to approve the funds, Trump signed a bill to reopen the federal government for three weeks, claiming to be optimistic that a compromise could be reached during that time.

The outcome of the longest government shutdown in U.S. history—35 days—was seen by many Trump supporters, along with much of the media, as a humiliating defeat for the president and a decisive victory for Nancy Pelosi and the Democrats. One government official volunteered that the shortfall of furloughed airline baggage checkers—some were unwilling to work without pay, others claimed they could not afford to come to work—posed "a level of risk that we cannot calculate." Trump's lack of concern for others and for the country became evident to many Americans who had previously managed to ignore their president's selfish, destructive behavior. His approval rating fell from just over 40 percent to just under 35 percent in the wake of this gormless and callous act.

The New Yorker cover for the week of January 28— "Walled In," by John Cuneo—had Donald Trump sitting at his desk in the Oval Office, behind a brick wall he was constructing, brick by brick. The completed section of the wall, curved at both ends and covered by coiled barbed wire—the kind used on top of prison walls—is well over Trump's head.

In searing red against a background of medium blue, the *Atlantic's* March issue bore the title "Impeach," heralding Yoni Appelbaum's lead article, "It's Time to Judge the President's Fitness to Serve."

By this time, the media conversation about Donald Trump's presidency had changed from there's no way he's impeachable to we need to give impeachment a shot.

Michael Cohen's Testimony Before the House Oversight Committee

Things became direr on February 27 when Michael Cohen, Trump's former lawyer and fixer, testified before the House Oversight Committee, chaired by Maryland Democrat Elijah Cummings (the "fixer" tag comes from novels and movies about organized crime). The next day, a six-column headline on page one in *The New York Times* exclaimed "Cohen Accuses Trump of Lies and Cover-ups." The story included an inset, with some of Cohen's most chilling quotes: "He is a racist. He is a con man. And he is a cheat"; "He asked me to pay off an adult film star, which I did"; "Mr. Trump knew of and directed the Trump Moscow negotiations throughout the campaign and lied about it. He lied about it because he never expected to win" (Ruiz, 2019).

These accusations had been bandied about over many months, but now we were hearing directly from someone who was under close congressional questioning and had been a participant in these events. Though he had previously lied in testimony before Congress, Cohen was now cooperating to reduce his sentence (to three years), and had nothing to gain by lying again, and everything to lose. He appeared, at times, to be stripping himself bare, painfully acknowledging how often he had lied for Donald Trump, and how many people he had threatened on orders from his boss.

For me, Cohen's most affecting revelations were these insights into Trump's character: "He is capable of behaving kindly, but he is not kind. He is capable of committing acts of generosity, but he is not generous. He is capable of being loyal, but he is fundamentally disloyal" (Li, 2019). Under pressure, the malignant narcissist shows flashes of kindness, generosity and loyalty, but only on occasions when doing so is beneficial to his overall plan of self-aggrandizement, or as a temporizing move when he is in a jam. In fact, overall, Donald Trump is nasty, cheap and lacks even the basic notion of what it means to be loyal to someone else—in his home life, his business dealings or in politics.

Cohen let it be known that Trump often threatened those whom he was hoping to persuade. He testified that he was aware of approximately 500 incidents where his boss had made threats, either directly or indirectly through his agents, promising to come down hard on the schools he attended if information about his SAT scores or academic performance leaked out. Trump has bragged about how diligently he worked on school assignments, what a good student he was and how high his IQ is.

During the Cohen hearings, Trump was in Hanoi meeting with Kim Jon Un. His attempt to trade a reduction in U.S. sanctions for Korea's promise of "denuclearization" quickly blew up, and he left a day early. *The New York Times* concluded an article titled "Trump-Kim Talks Undone by Big Egos and Bad Bets": "In the end, Mr. Trump flew back to Washington with nothing—no agreement on a peace declaration, and no ban on producing more nuclear fuel—meaning the North's arsenal will keep expanding while the two sides argue. There were only promises to keep talking" (Sanger & Wong, 2019). Trump had once again come up short on the world stage.

After Michael Cohen's testimony, in his concluding remarks, House Oversight Committee chairman Elijah Cummings declared: ". . . we are better than this. We really are. As a country, we are so much better than this." But are we, really? And who are "we" here? Trump's poll ratings rose to 46% after he returned from Hanoi. How much better than Trump and Cohen are the Americans who still approved of what this president had done in Hanoi and continues to do.

Several days after the House Oversight hearings, in a *New York Times* article titled "Donald Trump's Phony America," Frank Bruni declared: "This isn't just the land of the fraud but the home of the knave . . . . It takes two to bamboozle: the illusionist and the enraptured" (Bruni, 2019).

A sufficient number of Americans bought into Trump's lies for him to win the electoral majority in 2016. After the Cohen hearings, 46% of them still backed him.

Former FBI director James Comey, fired on May 9, 2017 by Trump for refusing to abort an investigation into the possibility that Trump's advisors conspired with Russia to influence the 2016 election, was in a good position to see how this president corrupts just about everyone who comes into his circle, and under his sway:

> Mr. Trump eats your soul in small bites. It starts with your sitting silent while he lies, both in public and private, making you complicit by your silence. In meetings with him, his assertions about what "everyone thinks" and what is "obviously true" wash over you, unchallenged— as they did at our private dinner on Jan. 27, 2017—because he's the president and he rarely stops talking. As a result, Mr. Trump pulls all of those present into a silent circle of assent.

Speaking rapid-fire with no spot for others to jump into the conversation, Mr. Trump makes everyone a co-conspirator in his preferred set of facts, or delusions. I have felt it—this president building with his words a web of alternative reality and busily wrapping it around all of us in the room (Comey, 2019).

James Comey wrote this assessment of his former boss' toxic character shortly after Attorney General William Barr issued a brief summary of the Robert Mueller Report that was widely seen as significantly distorting Mueller's findings in favor of Barr's boss, Donald Trump.

11

How Trump Might Respond to the Threat of Impeachment

Donald Trump's presidency is the most fulminant political psychodrama this country has had to endure so far. The prospect that someone with his unrestrained and depraved life trajectory will eventually have a catastrophic fall increases with time. Considering how uncivilly pathological narcissists and malignant narcissists take rejection and defeat (Muller, 2011), we need to be concerned about how Donald Trump might react if he had to face the full consequences of the damage he has done to this country and to the office he holds, particularly if he were to be forced out of the Oval Office through impeachment, or just threatened with impeachment.

The faultfinders would include voters to whom he made promises that were not kept, or promises that were kept but backfired; Democrats who see him as an incompetent gatecrasher and saboteur; Republicans who see him as a wrecker of their party; and close family members whom he has unaccountably drawn into his presidency who will likely be hurt in ways that we can only imagine.

Years ago, Trump stopped building the hotels, casinos and golf courses that became his trademark and began selling the Trump brand instead. Many of the products and projects he endorsed have failed, some spectacularly. In this and other counties, franchisees of Trump hotels, and other Trump enterprises have removed his name from buildings and mastheads. If Trump's presidency ends in a flame-out, the value of his name and brand would decline further, and the House of Trump would significantly contract.

If this happens, there is no way to predict how much Trump would deteriorate psychically, or what destructive fury he might unleash on those he felt had contributed to his fall. Attempting to reclaim some semblance of prelapsarian times, decompensating malignant narcissists often strike back at those they hold responsible for shattering their internal self-image, the pathological template on which their earlier, more successful lives depended (Muller, 2011).

At some point in Trump's descending course, I picture him sitting alone in the Oval Office looking down at his hyper-polished desktop, seeing nothing there but his own reflection, then looking up at a muted TV screen, with its steady flow of images from a formerly sycophantic Fox News, now documenting his undoing.

Narcissus, whose story was appropriated from Greek mythology by the Roman poet Ovid in the *Metamorphoses*, comes to mind. After having heartlessly rebuffed everyone who sought his friendship, we find Narcissus staring into a forest pool, absorbed in his own image, totally isolated. His tragic dilemma was that if he were to stand up and walk out of the forest—giving himself a shot at an authentic life—he would be forced to relinquish the watery self-image he had come to value above anyone or anything (Ovid, 1964, pp. 67-73).

Trump may eventually face a dilemma similar in form to that experienced by Narcissus, who was a pathological narcissist but not, as far as we know, a malignant one. Facing the unravelling of his presidency, Trump would almost certainly be reluctant to relinquish his twisted internal image of a "Great America," starring himself as its supreme asset and top dog, or the persona he partially derives from that image, the face he presents to the world. Charles M. Blow has recognized the brittleness of this structure: "One of Trump's greatest fears and greatest insecurities is being embarrassed and being exposed. Trump is petrified that someone will remove the mask he has been crafting for seven decades, or having it be revealed that that mask is made of paper rather than steel" (Blow, 2018).

Trump is and always has been mostly his mask. If exposed and held accountable for his actions to the point where this persona can no longer be sustained, the degree to which he might implode or explode is anyone's guess.

In May 2019, *The New York Times* published the results of a deep-dive investigation into Donald Trump's federal tax returns, from 1985-1994. The article was titled: "Decade in the Red: Trump Tax Figures Show Over $1 Billion in Business Losses":

By the time his master-of-the-universe memoir "Trump: The Art of the Deal" hit bookstores in 1987, Donald J. Trump was already in deep financial distress, losing tens of millions of dollars on troubled business deals, according to previously unrevealed figures from his federal income tax returns.

Mr. Trump was propelled to the presidency, in part, by a self-spun narrative of business success and of setbacks triumphantly overcome. He has attributed his first run of reversals and bankruptcies to the recession that took hold in 1990. But 10 years of tax information obtained by The New York Times paints a different, and far bleaker, picture of his deal-making abilities and financial condition (Buettner & Craig, 2019).

The gist of this long article is that Trump was far from the dealmaker he makes himself out to be, and that his real estate empire was nowhere as extensive, or as stable, as he claimed all along. A good deal of what Trump bought, sold and operated over the years turned out to rest on quicksand. The mask he showed to everyone, everywhere, was full of holes. The man who wanted everyone to believe that he was in full control was, in fact, perpetually out of control.

Sensing Trump's lack of respect for limits and boundaries, in business, politics and everything else, Philip Roth, who had demonstrated in his novels an extraordinary ability to plumb the depths of the human psyche, remarked to a friend: "What is most terrifying is that he

[Trump] makes any and everything possible" (Williams, 2018). These are simple, but chilling words. More than once, Trump asked his national security advisors why, if the U.S. has nuclear weapons, they are not used.

Trump's sociopathy—his disregard of all ethical and social norms—is a pivot point for both his malignant narcissism and his dangerousness, which are, ultimately, inseparable. Saying that Donald Trump is a malignant narcissist—and formally making that diagnosis—amounts to naming the universal elements of his pathological character *and* describing the kind of person he is. Outed and busted, this *is* Trump's *different existence* (van den Berg, 1972).

With admirable concision, historian Greg Grandin has captured some repeatedly exhibited, rebarbative facets of Trump's personality: notably, he says, Trump "cultivates a petulant hedonism, an unchecked freedom to hate, an enraged refusal of constraints" (Grandin, 2019). The diagnosis of malignant narcissism captures the totality of Donald Trump's biological inheritance, every influence he was exposed to and every response he made to these experiences.

Allen Frances, chairperson of the DSM-IV Task Force, has argued, unconvincingly as far as I am concerned, that Trump is not a malignant narcissist because his actions as president do not appear to adversely affect *him* (Frances, 2017). Granted, it is difficult to gage the narcissist's interior turmoil. Under pressure, even crumbling defenses permit narcissists to retain the illusion of being in control and of winning, even as they strain to maintain a compensatory persona, and feel threatened underneath their false bravura. As they decompensate and others become victims of their destructive revenge, they can often hide their pain, up to a point. Like so many malignant narcissists before him, Donald Trump is likely to be consumed in the chaos he created and which he has thrived on for so long, as he is being held to the laws that he always felt did not apply to him, and continually flouted.

12

Coda

Clinicians distinguish between diagnosing a mental illness and evaluating dangerousness. If evidence is forthcoming from a patient's interview, or from another source, that he or she is at risk for harming others, this determination triggers the clinician's "duty to warn" any likely target of that person's violence. Clinicians, myself included, who see Trump's first two years in office as one dangerous gambit after another and who know the potential for violence in those whose narcissism is malignant have a duty to warn not just an individual or two, but an entire country, and a world beyond that. How does someone in this position *not* try to spell out the danger Trump so obviously poses?

Donald Trump's conduct derives from a deeply entrenched character pathology that is notoriously resistant to treatment and attenuation. His narcissistic defenses have become so much a part of him that he is unwilling and/or unable to act on the evidence presented, from many sources, that what he is doing is not countenanced by anyone but himself and his staunchest followers (many of whom are acting primarily out of self-interest, or fear) and may lead to his downfall.

Trump's entrenched narcissistic defenses fend off insight, which, in those with less profound pathologies, can inspire the mitigation of a self-destructive course. His incompetent and dangerous presidency cannot be fully understood without grasping that he is acquiescing, moment by moment, to an array of long-standing psychodynamic defenses collectively known as malignant narcissism. Ultimately, this diagnosis and the recognition of the meaning of his behavior point to the same phenomenon.

Trump recognizes the difference between what is right and wrong, legal and illegal, and is therefore responsible for his actions before the law, even as he believes that he is above being held to these distinctions. If he is impeached (Leonhardt, 2019; Goldberg, 2019a; Witcover, 2019; Dionne, 2019), it should be because what he has done and not done since January 20, 2017—*how he has pathologically misused his freedom*—shows that he is unfit, psychologically and otherwise, to be president of the United States and Leader of the Free World, and because he rates a psychiatric diagnosis which, ipso facto, rules him out for holding high office. What we have seen so far from his rogue presidency, with its eerie resemblance to reality TV and psychodrama, portends even greater, and more dangerous lunacies.

13

The Mueller Report

In May 2017, Robert S. Mueller III was appointed special counsel to investigate Donald Trump's possible collusion with Russia's widely recognized interference in the 2016 presidential election, and Trump's subsequent efforts to stymie investigations into this inquiry. Mueller handed over his completed report to Attorney General William P. Barr on March 22, 2019.

Barr Summary of the Mueller Report

On March 24, Barr released what he claimed was a summary of Mueller's findings: there was no evidence that Trump had colluded with Russia's flagrant attempts to influence the 2016 election; Mueller had declined to rule on whether or not there was sufficient evidence to charge Trump with obstruction of justice for his efforts to limit the investigations of the FBI and the special counsel—in other words, to make a "traditional prosecutorial judgment" (Savage, 2019a). Attorney General Barr subsequently could have decided to charge Trump with obstruction of justice but declined to do so.

Trump claimed "complete and total exoneration," but it was quickly pointed out by the Democrats and the media that this was not the case: Mueller had *not cleared* Trump of the obstruction of justice charges. Democrats, many stunned by Barr's summary, reminded everyone that other investigations into Trump's irregular behavior, before and after he was elected president, were ongoing in Congress and in the civil courts.

Trump seemed to have dodged a bullet from the Mueller investigation, though he was by no means in the clear. Even if he were to win another term in 2020, he would still be open to impeachment if the evidence of malfeasance in his past acts became conclusive, or if he were to commit new impeachable offenses while in office. If he failed to get the Republican nomination in 2020, lose the general election or chose not to run for a second term, he would be subject to indictment by civil courts on a number of issues that have been brought to light by the media.

Newly emboldened by his "exoneration," Trump angrily lashed out at his accusers, saying *they* should now be investigated, and punished. He promised, once again, to rid the country of Obamacare, an action which, if taken, would have the immediate effect of leaving millions of Americans without health insurance.

Feeling exonerated, Donald Trump seemed likely to succumb to his worst instincts, putting himself in danger of being called out for the deviant acts he might still perpetrate as president. Something similar happened with Richard Nixon.

Riding the crest of an election mandate, Nixon gave full reign to the paranoia that tainted most of his career, ultimately ordering the break-in of the Democratic National Committee office on June 17, 1972, an event that exploded into the scandal that came to be known as Watergate. After two years of investigations, there was irrefutable proof that he instigated the Watergate breach and encouraged the five Watergate burglars to lie about what they had done. Caught out and facing certain impeachment, Nixon resigned on August 9, 1974.

As Donald Trump was pompously claiming exoneration and shrilly restating his claim that the special counsel's investigation had been a "witch hunt" all along, he may have been unaware that, on March 27, Robert Mueller had written a letter to Attorney General Barr objecting to the way Barr characterized the committee's conclusions. "The summary letter the Department [of Justice] sent to Congress and released to the public late in the afternoon of March 24 did not fully capture the context, nature, and substance of this Office's work and conclusions . . . . There is now public confusion about critical aspects of the results of our investigation. This threatens to undermine a central purpose for which the Department appointed the special counsel: to assure full public confidence in the outcome of the investigations" (Mr. Mueller's Letter to Mr. Barr, May 2, 2019).

Clearly, Robert Mueller was taking issue with the way Barr synopsized the special counsel's report. He also took issue with the timing of the release. According to the *New York Times* editorial, Mueller "had prepared detailed and accurate summaries of the two volumes of the report, one on contacts between the Trump campaign and Russian operatives, the second on potential obstruction of justice." In other words, Mueller had *already* synopsized his report: "Accordingly, the enclosed documents are in a form that can be released to the public consistent with legal requirements and Department policies. I am requesting that you provide these materials to Congress and authorize their public release at this time" (Mr. Mueller's Letter to Mr. Barr, May 2, 2019). At "this time," Mueller specified, not three weeks later.

The Full (Redacted) Mueller Report

On April 18, Attorney General William Barr released the eagerly anticipated full Mueller report, with redactions (Mueller, 2019a). Standing before TV cameras and a small contingent of reporters, Barr repeated the avowals of his March 24 summary, adding little to what had already been said. As expected, this attorney general protected his president, cherry-picking and right-spinning the 448-page document.

The next day, also as expected, *The New York Times* took a different tack, shifting the emphasis from the possible collusion of Trump with the Russian interference in the 2016 campaign to the corruption that Trump initiated from the White House during the two-year special counsel's investigation. The page-one *Times* headline for April 19 read: "MUELLER REPORT LAYS OUT

RUSSIAN CONTACTS AND TRUMP'S FRANTIC EFFORTS TO FOIL INQUIRY." Below the headline, in boxed black-on-yellow text, were seven out-takes from the report:[5]

1. Obstruction of justice remains an open question (Vol. II, p. 182)

"If we had confidence after a thorough investigation of the facts that the president clearly did not commit obstruction of justice, we would so state. Based on the facts and the applicable legal standards, we were unable to reach that judgement." [In *The Mueller Report* (2019a), the next sentence is: "Accordingly, while this report does not conclude that the President committed a crime, it also does not exonerate him."]

2. Trump tried to undermine the investigation, but his staff didn't go along (Vol. II, p. 158)

"The president's efforts to influence the investigation were mostly unsuccessful, but that is largely because the persons who surrounded the president declined to carry out orders or accede to his requests."

3. Trump's frequently faulty memory limited responses to the inquiry (appendix C, p. 1)

"We received the president's written responses in late November 2018 . . . . We noted, among other things, that the president stated on more than 30 occasions that 'he does not recall' or 'remember' or have an 'independent recollection' of information called for by the questions. Other answers were 'incomplete or imprecise.'"

4. No evidence of conspiracy despite the campaign's interests in Russia's offers (Vol. I, p. 173)

"The investigation established multiple links between Trump campaign officials and individuals tied to the Russian government. Those links included Russian offers of assistance to the campaign . . . . Ultimately, the investigation did not establish that the campaign coordinated or conspired with the Russian government in its election-interference activities."

5. Lies impeded the inquiry into possible Russian interference (Vol. I, p. 9)

"The investigation established that several individuals affiliated with the Trump campaign lied to the office, and to Congress, about their interactions with Russian-affiliated individuals and related matters. Those lies materially impaired the investigation of Russian election interference."

6. Mueller contends that Congress can charge a president with obstruction (Vol. II, p. 8)

"The conclusion that Congress may apply the obstruction laws to the president's corrupt exercise of the powers of office accords with our constitutional system of checks and balances and the principle that no person is above the law."

7. Trump thought Mueller's appointment would ruin his presidency (Vol. II, p. 78)

"When Sessions told the president that a special counsel had been appointed, the president slumped back in his chair and said, 'Oh my God. This is terrible. This is the end of my presidency.'"
[In *The Mueller Report* (2019a), the sentence "I'm fucked" appears immediately after this last sentence.]

The full quote gives every indication that Donald Trump knew, from the beginning, that he had something to fear from this investigation, in spite of his many blustering protestations to the contrary.

Quinta Jurecic has spelled out the significance of several of Trump's more hard-to-pin-down transgressions named in the Mueller report, including his public invitation to Russia to pursue Hillary Clinton's "missing" emails, Paul Manafort's sharing of poling data from the 2016 election with Russian operative Konstantin Kilimnik and the request Trump made of his former campaign manager Corey Lewandowsky to convey to Attorney General Jeff Sessions his wish that Mueller not investigate allegations of Russian interference in that election—a favor Lewandowski refused to do (Jurecic, 2019).

The conclusions drawn in the redacted version of the full Mueller report, bolstered by the analytical commentary that followed, made it harder—though certainly not impossible—for Donald Trump to claim "complete and total exoneration," as he did immediately after Attorney General Barr released his four-page summary of the report on March 24. But the most consequential upshot of the report, going forward, was that Congress had been issued a tacit invitation to continue its investigations and to debate the question of whether Trump's behavior merited impeachment.

Immediately after the redacted Mueller report was released, articles about the dangers of *not* impeaching Trump began to appear alongside those touting the disadvantages of moving in that direction. Charles Blow, who has written often against Donald Trump, titled a *New York Times* op-ed "Impeach Donald Trump?"

> [There] is no such thing as a failed impeachment. Impeachment exists separately from removal. Impeachment in the House is akin to an indictment, with the trial, which could convict and remove, taking place in the Senate. The Senate has never once voted to convict. So, an impeachment vote in the House has to this point been the strongest rebuke America is willing to give a president. I can think of no president who has earned this rebuke more than the current one . . . . I worry that inaction enshrines that idea that the American president is above America's laws. I worry that silent acquiescence bends our democracy toward monarchy, or dictatorship (Blow, 2019a).

The day before the Blow article appeared, an op-ed by another *Times* columnist, Michelle Goldberg, asked "Why Aren't We on the Road to Impeachment?"

Numerous commentators have said that the [Mueller] report reads like a road map for impeachment, and in a remotely functional country that's what it would be. Mueller makes it clear that because of the Office of Legal Council's opinion that a sitting president cannot be indicted, 'we determined not to apply an approach that could potentially result in a judgment that the President committed crimes.' Instead, the evidence is laid out for congressional action, or even for prosecutors to indict Trump after he leaves office (Goldberg, 2019a).

That same day, April 22, Nancy Pelosi said at her weekly news conference that the House of Representatives should continue their investigations into Trump's behavior, but not open a formal impeachment inquiry. Pelosi's recommendation was an appeal to get the facts first, then see if there is a case to be made for impeachment. House investigators were in a good position to start with the facts that Mueller and his team had already established, during a nearly two-year inquiry into Trump's efforts to obstruct justice. The *New York Times* national security and legal correspondent Charlie Savage culled the following six disclosures from Mueller's longer list of the president's obstructions (Savage, 2019b):

- Trump tried to fire Mueller [Vol. 2, pp. 77-90]
- Trump pushed McGahn [Donald F. McGahn II, former White House counsel] to deny the attempt to fire Mueller [Vol 2, pp. 113-120]
- Trump encouraged Manafort not to cooperate [Vol. 2, pp. 122-123]
- Trump tried to gut the investigation [Vol. 2, 90-98]
- Trump urged Comey to drop the Flynn investigation [Vol. 2, pp. 24-48]
- Trump fired Comey [Vol. 2, pp. 62-77] (Mueller, 2019a).

Congress and the courts now have to decide whether someone who did these things, and other things as well, should continue to be president of the United States, or be removed from office. If Trump is impeached by the House, but the Senate refuses to convict him, he would undoubtedly spin this outcome as *his* victory when campaigning for a second term. That risk must be weighed against the chance that, if Trump serves out his first term, he could win the 2020 election and be president for another four years. Such is Congress' dilemma, and ours.

Robert Mueller's Press Conference, May 29, 2019

On May 29, reading from a prepared text to an audience of reporters at the Justice Department, Robert Mueller appeared to confirm the widespread feeling that Attorney General William Barr had misrepresented the conclusions of the special counsel's full redacted report that was issued on April 18. His subdued recitation lasted barely ten minutes, and bore no surprises:

> [U]nder longstanding department policy, a president cannot be charged with a federal crime while

he is in office. That is unconstitutional. Even if the charge is kept under seal and hidden from public view, that, too, is prohibited. A special counsel's office is part of the Department of Justice, and by regulation, it was bound by that department policy. Charging the president with a crime was therefore not an option we could consider . . . .

[T]he Constitution requires a process other than the criminal justice system to formally accuse a sitting president of wrongdoing (Mueller, 2019b).

As to why the special counsel and his team declined to charge the president with one or more crimes—in spite of the considerable evidence they had uncovered during their investigation that could have influenced that decision—Mueller offered this amplification: "And beyond department policy, we were guided by principles of fairness. It would be unfair to potentially—it would be unfair to potentially accuse somebody of a crime when there can be no court resolution of the actual charge" (Mueller, 2019b).

Some will find this explanation convincing, others will not. No law prevented Mueller from pronouncing judgments about Trump's guilt or innocence. The fact is, he chose not to do so. He also declined to explicitly weigh in on whether the House should take up the question of impeachment, saying in effect, that was their call.

Robert Mueller's House Testimony, July 24, 2019

Under subpoena, and with no apparent relish, Robert Mueller testified before both the House Judiciary Committee (Jerrold Nadler, chairman) and the House Intelligence Committee (Adam Schiff, chairman) on July 24, 2019. Those who had hoped Mueller's testimony would be a lively "movie" made from the rather dry 448-page *Mueller Report* (2019a)—widely believed to have been read by few Americans—got to see a dry movie. Mueller stuck to his promise not to go beyond the written text in his testimony. His answers were brief, with little elaboration or color, many limited to yes and no. The longer responses that he did make were halting and labored. He made no attempt to create an integrating narrative.

If, overall, House interrogators couldn't pry anything new from Mueller during his nearly seven hours of testimony, Jerrold Nadler did succeed in having Mueller confirm what he saw as Trump's 10 "discrete acts" to obstruct the committee's investigation (Mueller, 2019a; Rahn, 2019). Excerpts from the special counsel's report were projected on large flat screens. Nadler read clearly and emphatically from his own text, asking Mueller, slide by slide, if that had been his conclusion (Fandos, 2019).

Jerrold Nadler: *[T]he president has repeatedly claimed that your report found there was no obstruction and that it completely and totally* *exonerated him. But that is not what your report said, is it?*

Robert Mueller: *Right, that is not what the report said.*

Mueller's brief responses, often just "yes" or "no," came like knife thrusts in a noirish movie.

If the House Democrats' intention was to get Robert Mueller's public verbal imprimatur for his committee's report, that goal was met. It is no exaggeration to say that the lapidary words constituting Mueller's 10 obstruction charges shaped the truth about this significant facet of Trump's murky presidency.

On the White House lawn, shortly after the hearings ended, Donald Trump told reporters that the Democrats had just created one of the greatest disasters in history. Still no collusion, no obstruction, he said, squinting in the late afternoon sunlight. Earlier, he had tweeted: "No collusion. No obstruction. No impeachment. Shut the coup cabal down" (Shear & Fadulu, 2019)!

To Impeach, or Not to Impeach

Even those who believe that Donald Trump is actively courting impeachment—and feel in their gut he should be removed from office— see a dark side to a successful, or even to an unsuccessful effort to impeach him. Maureen Dowd has captured the essence of what is surely still a dilemma:

> The attempt to impeach Trump is one of the rare cases in which something obviously justified is obviously stupid . . . .
>
> An impeachment could return Trump to power. The highchair king from Fifth Avenue would exult in his victimhood and energize his always-ready-to-be aggrieved followers.
>
> It could also lead to Democrats losing the House as their moderates fall and help Republicans hold the Senate. No Republicans would vote for impeaching Trump and some Democrats might refuse as well. Even if the House acted, Mitch

McConnell would smother it in the Senate, just like he did Merrick Garland . . . .

Hillary Clinton's campaign focused on what a terrible person Trump is. It turned out that enough voters knew that and didn't care. They wanted a racist Rottweiler (Dowd, 2019).

This is how things stood in the midsummer of 2019: damned if you do impeach, damned if you don't.

October 15, 2019

The movement of the House of Representatives toward starting impeachment hearings in the matter of Donald J. Trump is tracked with the media quotes that follow in Chapter 14. The final decision to open formal inquiries came on September 24, 2019 (see pp. 152-153).

14

Donald J. Trump Defiling America: The Media Watch

Sometime during the spring of 2019, two and a half years into the Trump administration—an interval that included the release of The Mueller Report—America's thinking about whether this president should be, or even could be impeached pivoted. What had previously seemed wrong and impossible about removing Trump from office from that point on looked both possible and necessary. Imagining the prospect of having Trump in the White House for another five and a half years, many voters, elected officials and media commentators concluded it was *this* outcome that was unthinkable.

In the midsummer of 2019, with the text for *Trump's Pathological Presidency* completed and production of the Kindle Direct Publication (KDP) format underway, the final arc of this president's reign could not be foreseen—even as evidence of a blind destructiveness in much of what he was saying and doing was rapidly accumulating. This trend, which often pro-duced new tremors daily, was captured in the spoken and written words of many elected offi-cials who make our laws, and by journalists and analysts whose job it is to expose threats to our American democracy.

In this concluding chapter, confident that the case for the threat posed by Donald Trump's psychic pathology had been made, I elected to step aside, go silent, and invite the unme-diated commentary of others who were more intimately involved with his presidency than I was. Collectively, their observations play like a Greek chorus, forewarning an inevitable tragic outcome for this president, and possibly a similar fate for the rest of us as well.

⚔

"Trump is goading us to impeach him, that's what he's doing every single day. He's just taunting, taunting, taunting because he knows it would be divisive in the country. But he doesn't really care, he wants to solidify his base."
—Nancy Pelosi, USA Today, May 7, 2019

"For America to stay America, Trump has to be defeated."
—Thomas L. Friedman,
The New York Times, May 8, 2019

"It sounds like he is asking us to impeach him. He puts us in a position where we at least have to look at it."
—Elijah Cummings,
The New York Times, May 9, 2019

"But [Trump] may get us there. He certainly seems to be trying and maybe this is his perverse way of dividing us more . . . he thinks that's to his political advantage, but it's certainly not to the country's advantage . . . part of our reluctance is we are already a bitterly divided country and an impeachment process will divide us further."

—Adam Schiff, ABC's *This Week*, May 12, 2019

"Impeachment is a decision for down the road. But we have to get the facts. Ultimately, impeachment or not impeachment is a political act. And before you do it, the American people have to support it."

—Jerry Nadler, CNN, May 15, 2019

"Michigan GOP Rep. Justin Amash Saturday (May 18) said he had concluded President Donald Trump committed 'impeachable conduct' and accused Attorney General William Barr of intentionally misleading the public. Amash's comments recommending Congress pursue obstruction of justice charges against Trump were the first instance of a sitting Republican in Congress saying the President's conduct meets the 'threshold for impeachment.'"

—Eli Watkins and Kevin Bohn, CNN,
May 19, 2019

"The drumbeat among Democrats to begin impeachment proceedings against President Trump got a little louder on Tuesday, when former White House counsel Donald McGahn failed to appear before the House Judiciary Committee after Trump instructed him to defy a subpoena."

—Dylan Stableford and Christopher Wilson,
Yahoo News, May 21, 2019

"I think it may be time at least to begin the process through the (House) Judiciary Committee

to determine whether or not there are impeachment proceedings."
—Bernie Sanders, interview with Jake Tapper, CNN's "The Lead," May 22, 2019

"For now, a majority of House Democrats seem inclined to support court efforts to uphold the various subpoenas and document requests before moving to impeachment. Giving Trump more time for Rose Garden and Twitter antics could also allow him to make the case for impeachment far better than Democrats ever could on their own."
—E. J. Dionne, *Albuquerque Journal*, May 25, 2019

"In the next few months, the White House will complete the rollback of the most significant federal effort to curb greenhouse-gas emissions, initiated during the Obama administration. It will expand its efforts to impose

Mr. Trump's hard-line views on other nations, building on his retreat from the Paris accord and his recent refusal to sign a communiqué to protect the rapidly melting Arctic region unless it was stripped of any references to climate change."

—Coral Davenport and Mark Landler, *The New York Times*, May 27, 2019

"[T]here were multiple, systematic efforts to interfere in our [2016 presidential] election. And that allegation deserves the attention of every American."

—Robert S. Mueller III, Justice Department press conference, May 29, 2019, as transcribed by *The New York Times*, May 30, 2019

"If the House Judiciary Committee deems it necessary [to start impeachment proceedings], I will support their decision."

—Bernie Sanders, Twitter, May 29, 2019

"The Mueller investigation has provided the evidence. It's up to Congress to examine that evidence and pursue justice to its conclusion."

—Seth Moulton, R-Mass., Twitter, via
The New York Times, May 30, 2019

"President Trump beckons us into the abyss of the hateful. The arc of his mind bends toward injustice . . . . Today . . . patriotism demands the defense of the Constitution, the rule of law, truth, freedom, human rights and the planet itself against the ravages issued from the Trump White House. Every day the American idea is sullied. Every day the distinction between truth and falsehood is undermined."

—Roger Cohen,
The New York Times, June 1, 2019

"I don't want to see him [Trump] impeached, I want to see him in prison."

—Nancy Pelosi, Politico, June 6, 2019

"To Serve Donald Trump is to lose all self-respect. You lie for him. You cover for him. You hate for him . . . . With William Barr, Trump now has an attorney general who doesn't care how much lasting damage he does to truth, justice and the American way. His mandate as the nation's top prosecutor is to carry out Trump's private vendettas."

—Timothy Egan,
The New York Times, June 8, 2019

"As House Speaker Nancy Pelosi opts to do more intimidating fact-finding before pulling the trigger, more and more House Democrats are calling for the impeachment process to begin. House Majority Leader Steny Hoyer of Maryland, while backing his speaker, has made it clear that he has heard them."

—Jules Witcover, *The Baltimore Sun*,
June 11, 2019.

"For two and a half years in office, Mr. Trump has spun out so many misleading or untrue statements about himself, his enemies, his policies, his politics, his family, his personal story, his finances and his interactions with staff that even his own former communications director once said 'he's a liar' and many Americans long ago concluded that he cannot be trusted."

—Peter Baker,
The New York Times, June 15, 2019

"President Donald Trump's re-election campaign is cutting ties with some of its own pollsters after leaked internal polling showed the president trailing former Vice President Joe Biden in critical 2020 battleground states, according to a person close to the campaign."
—Chuck Todd, Kristen Welker and Ben Kamisar,
NBC News, June 16, 2019

"Speaker Nancy Pelosi on Wednesday ruled out censuring President Donald Trump if the House doesn't impeach him, downplaying a less drastic censure as 'a day at the beach' for the president. Pelosi, D-Calif., told reporters at a breakfast sponsored by the Christian Science Monitor that censure would be 'just a way out' of House Democrats' efforts to see if Trump has committed impeachable offenses. 'If you're going to go, you ought to go. In other words, if the goods are there, you must impeach,' she said."
—Nancy Pelosi, *Associated Press*, June 19, 2019

"Legendary advice columnist E. Jean Carroll accused Donald Trump of raping her in the dressing room of a New York City department store some 23 years ago, joining more than a dozen women who have previously come forward with allegations of Trump›s sexual misconduct. Carroll—who said that Trump attacked her in a Bergdorf Goodman dressing room, pulled down her tights, and 'thrust his penis' in her—detailed the alleged incident in her upcoming book, What Do We Need Men For? A Modest Proposal, an excerpt of which was published in the Cut on Friday." (Trump denies the accusation and insisted he never even met his accuser.)

—Tasneem Nashrulla, BuzzFeed News,
June 21, 2019

"If anything in the second decade of the 21st century warrants impeachment of an American president, it should be this: Ignoring science and the harmful effects of climate change, and putting humanity at grave risk. That might not fit the bill under the Constitution, which allows impeachment for 'treason, bribery, or other high crimes and misdemeanors.' But the stubborn refusal to aggressively address climate change is a dangerous dereliction of duty that warrants a president's removal from office . . . .

Four or five years ago, I would never have seen such regressive action as warranting the removal of a chief executive. I would have seen it as a difference of opinion or ideology. Not anymore. Things have changed, and rapidly."
—Dan Rodricks, *The Baltimore Sun,*
June 23, 2019

"House Judiciary Committee Chairman Jerrold Nadler (D., N.Y.) and House Intelligence Committee Chairman Adam Schiff (D., Calif.) said that the special counsel had agreed to testify in open session on July 17 [later rescheduled for July 24] pursuant to a subpoena . . . . 'Americans have demanded to hear directly from the Special Counsel so they can understand what he and his team examined, uncovered, and determined about Russia's attack on our democracy, the Trump campaign's acceptance and use of that help, and President Trump and his associates' obstruction of the investigation into that attack,' the lawmakers wrote in a statement."

—Siobhan Hughes and Sadie Gurman,
The Wall Street Journal, June 26, 2019

"Today's political landscape presents an incongruous scene: Despite a strong economy—usually a good predictor of presidential popularity—President Trump's approval rating remains stuck in the low to mid-40s . . . . The American people have specific complaints about Mr. Trump's behavior, and about the character traits underlying it. Multiple surveys over the past year have found that most Americans regard the president as dishonest. Only 4 in 10 think he cares about people like them. A Gallup pole released last June showed only 35% of Americans saw the president as a person they admire, while only 31% viewed him as working across party lines to get things done. A Pew survey last October found that only 24% thought the president was 'even-tempered'; 70% said he wasn't."

—William A. Galston, *The Wall Street Journal*, June 26, 2019

"Former President Jimmy Carter said Friday morning that Donald Trump is an illegitimate president due to Russian interference in the 2016 election. Carter, 94, was speaking at a Carter Center event on human rights in Leesburg, Va., when he was asked how he would deal with Russian meddling in the last presidential election. 'The president himself should condemn it, admit that it happened, which I think 16 intelligence agencies have already agreed to say,' said Carter. 'And there's no doubt that the Russians did interfere in the election, and I think the interference although not yet quantified, if fully investigated would show that Trump didn't actually win the election in 2016. He lost the election, and he was put into office because the Russians interfered on his behalf.'"

—Christopher Wilson, Yahoo News,
June 28, 2019

"President Trump has invited the American people to what he claims will be the biggest and best Fourth of July celebration in the nation's history. Influenced by the huge nationalist displays he witnessed in Europe, Mr. Trump promises 'a really great parade to show our military strength.' And he will treat the country to a 'major fireworks display, entertainment and an address by your favorite President, me!'

All Americans should be appalled. Even during an era of extreme hyperbole, the unabashed narcissism driving the parade plans is astonishing. It runs counter to the explicit aims and faith of the ordinary Americans who founded the United States."

—T. H. Breen,
The New York Times, July 4, 2019

"During Thursday's Fourth of July celebration, Mr. Trump's cherished tanks were stationed in a 'static display,' because driving them into position would have damaged Washington's streets. A stationary display was all too fitting, for it is the most common posture of tanks on the modern battlefield. Like President Trump's false promises, they weren't going anywhere."

—Elliott D. Woods,

The New York Times, July 7, 2019

"In a series of leaked diplomatic cables, Britain's ambassador to the United States, Kim Darroch, described President Trump as 'radiating insecurity' and his administration as diplomatically 'clumsy and inept,' a withering assessment that threatened to damage bilateral relations at a delicate moment for Britain . . . .

The most closely held of the cables [sent between 2017 and the present] was intended as an update on the new Trump administration for a narrow audience of top British officials. It described the chaos inside the new administration, the concerns about the future of the Atlantic relationship and the struggle to figure out who had the president's ear.

It was unclear who leaked the documents and how The Mail [a British newspaper] obtained them . . . .

In the cables, the British ambassador says that British analysts do not believe that the Trump administration 'is going to become substantially more normal; less dysfunctional; less unpredictable; less faction riven; less diplomatically clumsy and inept' . . . .

[Mr. Darroch] warned of 'real risks on the horizon,' as Mr. Trump guided United States policy away from consensus with Britain. 'This America First administration could do some profoundly damaging things to the world trade system such as denounce the W.T.O., tear up existing trade details, launch protectionist action, even against allies,' he wrote. 'It could further undermine international action on climate change, or further cut U.N. funding.'"

—Ellen Barry,

The New York Times, July 8, 2019

"The House Judiciary Committee on Thursday [July 11] approved a dozen new subpoenas targeting a who's who of witnesses cited in Robert S. Mueller III's report. Democrats sought to elevate their showdown with President Trump over episodes of possible obstruction of justice documented by the special counsel . . . .

Among prominent figures to be subpoened by the Democrats are Jeff Sessions, the former attorney general; Rod J. Rosenstein, his deputy who appointed Mr. Mueller, the special counsel; John F. Kelly, the former White House chief of staff; Jared Kushner, the president's son-in-law and special advisor; and Cory Lewandowski, a former Trump campaign manager."

—Nicholas Fandos,

The New York Times, July 12, 2019

"President Trump said on Sunday that a group of four minority congresswomen feuding with Nancy Pelosi should 'go back' to the countries they came from rather than 'loudly and viciously telling the people of the United States' how to run the government.

Wrapped inside that insult, which was established as a racist trope, was a factually inaccurate claim: Only one of the lawmakers was born outside the country.

Even though Mr. Trump has repeatedly refused to back down from stoking racial divisions, his willingness to deploy a lowest-rung slur—one commonly and crudely used to single out the perceived foreignness of nonwhite, non-Christian people—was largely regarded as beyond the pale.

'So interesting to see Progressive Democrat Congresswomen who originally came from countries whose governments are a complete and total catastrophe, the worst, the most corrupt and inept anywhere in the world,' Mr. Trump wrote on Twitter, 'now loudly and viciously telling the people of the United States, the greatest and most powerful Nation on earth, how our government is to be run.'

Mr. Trump added: 'Why don't they go back and help fix the totally broken and crime infested places from which they came. Then come back and show us how it is done.'"

—Katie Rogers and Nicholas Fandos,
The New York Times, July 15, 2019

"President Trump woke up Sunday morning, gazed out at the nation he leads, saw the dry kindling of race relations and decided to throw a match on it. It was not the first time, nor is it likely to be the last. He has a pretty large carton of matches and a ready supply of kerosene.

His twitter harangue goading Democratic congresswomen of color to 'go back' to the country they came from, even though most of them [three out of four] were actually born in the United States, shocked many. But it should have surprised few who have watched the way he has governed a multicultural, multiracial country the last two and a half years.

When it comes to race, Mr. Trump plays with fire like no other president in a century. While others who occupied the White House at times skirted close to or even over the line, finding ways to appeal to the resentments of white Americans with subtle and not-so-subtle appeals, none of them in modern times fanned the flames as overtly, relentlessly and eagerly as Mr. Trump . . . .

He is only saying what others believe but are too afraid to say, he insists. And each time the flames roar and Mr. Trump tosses a little more accelerant on top. The fire may be hot, but that's the way he likes it."

—Peter Baker,
The New York Times, July 15, 2019

"A U. K. newspaper has published more lea-ked memos revealing a British ambassador's assessments of the Trump administration, including one in which the envoy to Washington said President Donald Trump pulled out of the Iran nuclear deal to spite predecessor Barack Obama."

—Jill Lawless, *Associated Press/The Baltimore Sun,*
July 15, 2019

"The obvious unifying element for Democrats looking ahead to the 2020 presidential election is their imperative to oust Donald Trump from the Oval Office. They desire it for a multitude of reasons, starting with his glaring incompetence for the job and the rampant corruption in his regime.

But if the campaign comes off as only a bitter vendetta against Mr. Trump, it will fail to identify the deep damage he has already inflicted on our constitutional brand of self-government with his autocratic ways.

His war on Congress in conflict with America's separation of powers among our co-equal executive, legislative and judicial branches is a direct and brutal assault on our small-'d' democratic system.

His blatantly illegal usurpation of the congressional power of the purse—raising and authorizing public money to run the country, including its vital military arm—should itself be an impeachable offense.

So should Mr. Trump's direction to administration officials to ignore congressional subpoenas for testimony, dealing with his various governmental and private-business activities. It first laughs off foreign intervention in our elections process and then skirts emolument prohibitions expressly barred by the Constitution.

In all this, the Trump presidency is an open attack on our cherished political principles across the board, for more than two years eroding and defiling them to the detriment of our standing on the world stage."

—Jules Witcover, *The Baltimore Sun,*
July 16, 2019

"Donald Trump insists he's not a racist. This is, increasingly, a bit beside the point. What is excruciatingly clear, and what matters most right now, is that he has chosen to ground his politics and his presidency in fomenting racial hatred. Whatever he may feel in his bones, he is an avid race warrior.

That is the meaning of the chant of 'Send her back! Send her back! Send her back!' that resounded at his rally in Greenville, N.C., on Wednesday evening. An arena full of President Trump's supporters roared these words after Mr. Trump aimed their animosity at Representatives Ilhan Omar of Minnesota, who immigrated from Somalia. He smeared her as trafficking in 'vicious anti-semitic screeds' and a left-wing radical who sympathizes with Al Qaeda, hates America and 'looks down with contempt on the hard-working Americans.'

As the xenophobic chant engulfed him, the president paused, basking in the moment. He then went on to attack the three other freshmen representatives—women of color, all—who are members of the so-called squad. He suggested that Rashida Tlaib of Michigan 'does not love' America and that Alexandria Ocasio-Cortez of New York had declared 'contemporary America—that's you, that's me, that's all of us'—to be 'garbage.'

The president is looking to divide Americans along color lines, to conjure a zero-sum vision of America in which whites must contend against nonwhites for jobs, wealth, safety and citizenship. He thinks this approach will win him another four years in the White House. At this point, does it much matter if he is acting purely out of political cynicism, with no element of personal prejudice? The rage he is nurturing and the pain he is causing are all too real. The damage he is doing will take years to undo."

—Editorial,
The New York Times, July 19, 2019

"[I]n America, the unimaginable is the new norm: a fully blossoming fascism. We're stuck in a hideous loop of hate. But it's also an idiocy loop."

—Timothy Egan,
The New York Times, July 20, 2019

"Surprise, surprise: Donald Trump has no bottom. Just when you think he has sunk as low as he can, he stages a rally like that atrocity in North Carolina on Wednesday night and sinks lower. But the key takeaway is not that he is a demagogue or a racist: These were facts put in evidence long ago. It is that Democrats cannot afford to take unnecessary risks, dream deferrable dreams and engage in avoidable distractions as they set about the urgent work of defeating him. The 2020 election isn't about getting everything that Democrats want and that Democrats deserve. It's about getting rid of Trump, because the price of not doing so could be this nation's very soul."

—Frank Bruni,
The New York Times, July 21, 2019

"If Trump has an unbreakable bond with his supporters, it's because he gives them permission to express their sense of siege. His rhetoric frees them from the mores and norms that keep their grievance in check. His rallies—his political carnivals—provide an opportunity to affirm their feelings in a community of like-minded individuals."

—Jamelle Boui,
The New York Times, July 21, 2019

"Democratic hopes are rising on an unlikely horse. Mr. Mueller has made his reluctance to testify widely known, and his appearance [before two House of Representatives committees on July 24] could easily backfire. If the hearings fail to sizzle, the viewing public could be left agreeing with the president that it is time to move on."

—Nicholas Fandos,
The New York Times, July 21, 2019

"There is no higher duty for Congress than to investigate and act when such a report [like Robert Mueller's] lands on your desk. Those who say 'oh, a Senate supermajority will never convict Trump' have it backward . . . . [O]ur Constitution allows the House to investigate without the worry that its investigation will be twisted for political ends that would force the removal of an innocent president. The members of the House have a duty to act even if the Senate won't convict, because they are setting the standards for future presidents and because impeachment hearings will crystallize the nation's attention on the actual events, as opposed to spin from the president and attorney general."

—Neal A. Katyal,
The New York Times, July 23, 2019

"'The Mueller book will never be read by most of the American public, but the Mueller movie will be watched,' Sen. Richard Blumenthal, D-Conn., said when it was announced that Mueller would testify before the congressional committees."

—Yahoo News, July 23, 2019

"After months of anticipation, Robert S. Mueller III, the former special counsel, delivered nearly seven hours of dry, sometimes halting testimony before Congress on Wednesday [July 24]. Republicans and Democrats sparred over his conclusions, but in back-to-back hearings, Mr. Mueller mostly reiterated the findings of his two-year investigation into Russian interference in the 2016 election without offering any dramatic new disclosures.

Mr. Mueller may have been reluctant to go beyond the four corners of his 448-page report, but with a series of one-word answers and short-winded darts, the former special counsel dealt a sharp blow to President Trump's version of events by broadcasting his own meticulous research.

Asked if Mr. Trump 'wasn't always being truthful' or complete in his written answers under oath to the special counsel's questions, Mr. Mueller responded, 'I would say generally' . . . .

Liberals who support opening impeachment proceedings against Mr. Trump had hoped that testimony by the former special counsel would finally electrify their efforts. The early verdict suggests that did not happen.

Mr. Mueller himself clearly did not want to let the term escape his mouth, nor did he provide the kind of shocking new evidence or analysis that would have forced the issue. When

Representative Mike Johnson, Republican of Louisiana, asserted that the special counsel's report did not recommend or even discuss impeachment, the witness would not even nod along.

'I am not going to talk about that issue,' Mr. Mueller said."

—Nicholas Fandos,
The New York Times, July 25, 2019.

"'Much as I hate to say it, this morning's hearing [before the House Judiciary Committee] was a disaster,' Laurence Tribe, the Harvard law professor who has argued that the House should pursue impeachment, wrote on Twitter. 'Far from breathing life into his damning report, the tired Robert Mueller sucked the life out of it. The effort to save democracy and the rule of law from this lawless president has been set back, not advanced.'"

—Peter Baker,
The New York Times, July 25, 2019

"House Speaker Nancy Pelosi, D-Calif., said Friday that a decision on whether the House pursues the impeachment of President Donald Trump will be made in a 'timely fashion' and denied the idea that she is trying to 'run out the clock' on the issue.

'No, I'm not trying to run out the clock,' Pelosi said at her final weekly press conference before she departs Washington for the House's six-week summer recess.

Asked how long the Democrats' court fight might take, Pelosi would not lay out a timeline. 'We will proceed when we have what we need to proceed—not one day sooner,' she said.

Democrats are seeking to enforce in court subpoenas for certain documents in their investigation as well as testimony from witnesses, all of which the administration has not complied with. This includes requests for six years of the president's tax returns."

—Rebecca Shabad, NBC News, July 26, 2019

"President Trump lashed out at a leading African-American congressman on Saturday, calling him 'a brutal bully' who represents a Baltimore-based district that has become a 'disgusting, rat and rodent infested mess' where 'no human being would want to live.'

Mr. Trump's attack on Representative Elijah E. Cummings, a Democrat from Maryland and leading critic of the president, parroted a segment that aired earlier in the morning on 'Fox & Friends.' The president suggested that the congressman was a hypocrite for criticizing conditions in migrant detention centers at the southwestern border when his own district is blighted. Mr. Trump also made a vague and unsubstantiated insinuation of corruption.

'Rep. Elijah Cummings has been a brutal bully, shouting and screaming at the great men & women of Border Patrol about conditions at the Southern Border, when actually his Baltimore district is FAR WORSE and more dangerous,' Mr. Trump wrote. 'His district is considered the Worst in the USA.' He went on: 'Cummings' district is a disgusting, rat and rodent infested mess. If he spent more time in Baltimore, maybe he could help clean up this very dangerous & filthy place.'

Mr. Cummings responded on Twitter shortly afterword, saying he was a vigorous advocate for his district. 'Mr. President, I go home to my district daily,' he wrote. 'Each morning, I wake up, and I go and fight for my neighbors.'"

—Peter Baker,

The New York Times, July 28, 2019

"Testifying before Congress last week about his investigation of Russian interference in the 2016 elections, Robert Mueller, the former special counsel, seemed eager—desperate, even—to drive home one message: foreign adversaries are intent on undermining American democracy, and the United States is still vulnerable to them.

Even as Mr. Mueller declined to elaborate on most of his findings, he was unequivocal in warning that Russia meddled in the 2016 presidential race, that it aims to do so again—'They're doing it as we sit here,' he said—and that 'many more countries' are developing similar capabilities. Declaring foreign inter-ference 'among the most serious' challenges to American democracy, he urged those with 'responsibility in this area' to act 'swiftly.'

—Editorial,
The New York Times, July 28, 2019

"Last Wednesday, after Robert Mueller's terse and sometimes halting congressional testi-mony, conventional wisdom quickly congealed: Mueller's performance had made Donald Trump's impeachment far less likely . . . .

Less than a week later, it's clear that these hot takes were wrong. At no point in Trump's wretched rule has impeachment appeared more probable. Indeed, Democrats on the House

Judiciary Committee, which would oversee impeachment hearings, argue that an inquiry into impeachment has already begun. An inexorable confrontation between the House and the president has been set in motion . . . .

Mueller's presentation may have been underwhelming, but he allowed Democrats to put a bow around his findings, clearing away some of the deliberate confusion created by Attorney General William Barr's misleading summary. 'The press focused on the performance and the optics instead of on the substance,' said Jerry Nadler, chairman of the Judiciary Committee . . . .

[J]ust as Trump's recent racial outbursts forced renewed attention to his bigotry, Mueller made Congress squarely confront the president's perfidy. Once he testified, Democrats could no longer punt on the impeachment question by saying that they were waiting to hear from him."

—Michelle Goldberg,
The New York Times, July 30, 2019

"We know who President Donald Trump is talking to when he lobs his racist taunts: his right-wing base. He's talking to working-class, mostly white voters who think that everything is being taken from them and that immigrants and African Americans are to blame. Playing the race card fires them up and, Mr. Trump is calculating, will bring them to the polls.

However many such people exist, he will get their votes. Not much is going to change their minds. Not his broken promise to save the coal industry, the damage he did to farmers with tariffs or his massive tax cuts for the rich. They'll turn a blind eye to all his flaws as long as he heaps the blame on others—the media, coastal elites and especially minorities and immigrants. As long as the president plays into their insecurities, he can do no wrong. And other Republican lawmakers will fall in line, as they have done time and again, to ride that wave support."

—Editorial, *The Baltimore Sun*, July 31, 2019

"'Some suggest that the Senate is highly unlikely to convict the president should the House impeach him and that his chances of re-election will therefore be enhanced,' Representative Denny Heck [D-WA] said. 'That may be true. What is truer is that nothing less than the rule of law is at stake.'"

—Nicholas Fandos,
The New York Times, August 2, 2019

"[T]he Mueller report may turn out to be more of a film noir than anything else. The detective successfully uncovers the plot, only to discover that the society around him is too rotten to do anything about it. For all the missing pieces in this story, the issue is less whether it can be told and more whether anyone cares to listen."

—Quinta Jurecic,
The New York Times, August 3, 2019.

"[Trump is] a moral arsonist, and if he determined that the only way to hold on to power was to burn everything to the ground, he'd gladly be king of ashes. To paraphrase Milton: Better to reign over a ruined country than to be just another crass plutocrat in a noble one."

—Frank Bruni,
The New York Times, August 7, 2019

"Trump lashed out at Fox on Wednesday morning, accusing the network in tweets of 'heavily promoting the Democrats,' and adding, 'The New @FoxNews is letting millions of GREAT people down! We have to start looking for a new News Outlet. Fox isn't working for us anymore!'"

—Paul Farhi and John Wagner,
The Washington Post, August 28, 2019

"Trump is a man who has been progressively hollowed out by the acid of his own self-regard."

—David Brooks, *The New York Times*,
August 30, 2019

"Donald Trump's genius was, as it so often is, his inability to dissemble: no one can quite believe what he gets away with because we assume that a public act is unlikely to be incriminating. We interpret as strut and boasting what is actually a confession. Richard Nixon, a genuinely Shakespearean villain, had full knowledge of his wrongdoing and a bad conscience about it, if not enough of one. Trump is a figure right out of the Theatre of Cruelty; he just acts out, without any mental interior workings, aside from narcissistic necessity."

—Adam Gopnik, *The New Yorker,*
September 2, 2019

"Joe Biden accused Donald Trump of abusing the power of his presidency in urging the Ukrainian President to investigate Biden's son, Hunter, to smear his presidential campaign, angrily calling on Congress to investigate Trump's contact with the foreign leader. 'This appears to be an overwhelming abuse of power to get on the phone with a foreign leader who is looking for help from the United States and ask about me and imply things if that's what happened, that appears to be what happened . . . This is outrageous,' the former vice president and 2020 Democratic candidate told reporters on Saturday before attending the Polk County Democrats Steak Fry in Des Moines, Iowa."
—Caroline Kelly, CNN, September 22, 2019

"Elizabeth Warren on Friday evening sent out a series of tweets that, in addition to calling out Donald Trump for his criminality, rebuked Congress for enabling him. 'After the Mueller report, Congress had a duty to begin impeachment,' wrote Warren. 'By failing to act, Congress is complicit in Trump's latest attempt to solicit foreign interference to aid him in U.S. elections. Do your constitutional duty and impeach the president.'"

—Michelle Goldberg,
The New York Times, September 23, 2019

"Speaker Nancy Pelosi announced on Tuesday that the House would begin a formal impeachment inquiry of President Trump, saying that he had betrayed his oath of office and the nation's security in seeking to enlist a foreign power for his own political gain. 'The actions taken to date by the president have seriously violated the Constitution,' she said after emerging from a meeting of House Democrats in the basement of the Capitol. Mr. Trump, she

said, 'must be held accountable—no one is above the law.'"

—Nicholas Fandos,
The New York Times, September 24, 2019

Nancy Pelosi's observation, made on May 7, 2019, that Donald Trump was "goading" and "taunting" the House of Representatives to impeach him (our first entry in the "Media Watch," see p. 112) appears to have come full circle.

Notes

[1]Once the reader gets past the first few pages in Chapter 4 of Fromm's *The Heart of Man* (pp. 59-90)—devoted to Freud's hydraulic explanation of narcissism—there is a fine overview of narcissism, malignant and otherwise.

[2]During the time that Adolf Meyer directed the Phipps Clinic at Johns Hopkins (1913-1941), he urged his residents to follow this approach in "formulating" a psychiatric diagnosis. The Hopkins psychiatry department continues to ply that path to this day (McHugh & Slavney, 1998; Chisolm & Lyketsos, 2012; Muller, 2018).

[3]Some writers who are not familiar with the discipline of phenomenology tend to be intuitive phenomenologists. In taking on a subject, they, in effect, carry out the phenomenologist's forced halt—the Epoché—bracketing much of what remains of the world while at the same time allowing some elements that contribute to the structure of the phenomenon under consideration to leak through the brackets. In their hands, the Epoché is a less systematic effort—not strictly subject to rules that produce the more rounded results phenomenologists strive for—but nonetheless accords pride of place to meaning and structure.

To illustrate what we are calling intuitive phenomenology, we will unpack two related descriptions of Donald Trump's aversion to what is consensually known as truth.

First: David Brooks sees through the "incompetence" that Trump often demonstrates: "the true genius at incompetence like our president flails and flounders and is too incompetent to recognize his own incompetence" (2007a). Brooks gets that Trump inhabits "a separate universe of negative information," and that this is not just a matter of telling lies, but points to something different about this man's existence that leads him to lie repeatedly, about anything and everything.

Brooks' intuition can be taken another step. Trump's perpetual disregard for truth may be rooted in a pathological psychic structure that has already been described here as a metaphorical "distorted internal mirror," fractured in such a way that the constancy of perception required for a stable and sustainable grasp of what is real and true—psychoanalysts call this "object constancy"—is impossible. Trump *appears* ignorant because everything that enters his consciousness is disconnected from the restraints of what most people think of as reality, so that "truth" can be anything he needs it to be. He operates out of a *different reality*, which is the ground of his different existence.

Second: A year before the Brooks article appeared, following a similar intuition, Maureen Dowd offered this way of understanding Trump's pathological lying: "Narcissists see only themselves in a fun-house mirror, either larger or smaller than they really are at any given moment, so it is impossible for others to convey a true picture to them" (Dowd, 2016). By distributing fragments of the truth of a given situation among many internal "mirrors," Trump can avoid the worse of the anxiety he would feel if he chose to go with only one version of that truth, in one mirror. Processing everything he experiences as *break it up and spread it out* is one way to understand the defense that makes Trump a pathological liar.

[4]Some clinicians have questioned whether narcissism is a mental illness, or just a collection of narcissistic traits (Malkin, 2017). We distinguish here between *productive narcissism*, a non-pathological condition, and *narcissistic*

personality disorder and *malignant narcissism*, which are both pathological conditions.

The dimensional model of pathological narcissism is a metaphorical spectrum consisting of sets of narcissistic traits of increasing pathological character—from narcissistic personality disorder through malignant narcissism—where, at certain points in the spectrum, continuity yields to discontinuity, and discrete phenomena may be discerned. In Meyerian psychiatry, a pathological trait amounts to a deeply engrained bad habit that originated in a maladaptive response to one or more anxiety-inducing events, usually experienced early in life, which has become part and parcel of someone's personality.

In *The Four Domains of Mental Illness* (Muller, 2018), the *phenomena* of narcissistic personality disorder and malignant narcissism are identified and characterized. These phenomena fall in the 2nd domain and come about in the context of aberrant personality development and temperament. Biological factors—always present in the healthy as well as the pathological human psyche—contribute as correlatives to these 2nd domain conditions but are not primary causes (pp. 76-77). When a sufficient number of narcissistic traits are present, to a sufficient degree, a psychobiological structural transformation of the psyche occurs. Together, these traits, along with their psychobiological correlates, constitute the phenomena of narcissistic personality disorder and malignant narcissism (pp. 127-135).

Narcissistic personality disorder and malignant narcissism are 2nd domain *mental illnesses*, not 4th domain *brain diseases*, which include *some* psychotic disorders (manifestations of delirium, biogenic schizophrenia) and *some* mood disorders (bipolar I disorder, but not bipolar II conditions or most unipolar depression). This parsing is different from that in the medical model of mental illness—the theoretical foundation for the DSM-5—which holds that *all* mental illnesses are brain diseases.

Some members of the DSM-5 Task Force lobbied hard to eliminate personality disorders, which were introduced in the DSM-III, from the DSM-5, claiming that these variations in human behavior were not "diagnoses." Their efforts obviously failed. Was the reluctance to see personality disorders as mental illnesses attributed to the improbability that the aberrations comprising narcissism, paranoia, histrionics, etc. have a demonstrable biological cause?

[5]The Scribner edition of *The Mueller Report* (2019a) is double-paginated. Pages from the original Mueller report that William Barr released to Congress and to the publishers of several different editions are centered at the bottom; those from the Scribner edition, which is cited here, are at the bottom right.

References

Baker, P. (2019). Self-made crisis and a predictable hero. *The New York Times*, June 9, 2019, pp. 1, 10.

Blow, C. M. (2017, Oct. 19). Trump isn't Hitler. But the lying . . . *The New York Times*. https://www.nytimes.com/2017/10/19/opinion/trump-isnt-hitler-but-the-lying.html

Blow, C. M. (2018, August 20). Nixon, Clinton and Trump. *The New York Times*, p. A19.

Blow, C. M. (2019a, April 22). Impeach Donald Trump? *The New York Times*, p. A23.

Blow, C. M. (2019b, May 6). Defending the free press. *The New York Times*, p. A23.

Brooks, D. (2017a, April 7). The coming incompetence crisis. *The New York Times*, p. A29.

Brooks, D. (2017b, Oct. 31). When politics becomes your idol. *The New York Times*, p. A23.

Brooks, D. (2019, Aug. 2). Listen to Marianne Williamson. *The New York Times*, p. A27.

Bruni, F. (2018, October 21). Donald Trump's perverse advantage. *The New York Times*, p. SR3.

Bruni, F. (2019, March 3). Donald Trump's phony America. *The New York Times*, p. SR3.

Buettner, R. & Craig, S. (2019). Decade in the red: Trump tax figures show over $1 billion in business losses. *The New York Times*, May 8, 2019, pp. A1, 14, 15.

Chisolm, M. S. & Lyketsos, C. G. (2012). *Systematic psychiatric evaluation: A step-by-step guide to applying "The perspectives of psychiatry."* Baltimore, MD: Johns Hopkins University Press.

Comey, J. (2019, May 2). How Trump co-opts leaders like Barr. *The New York Times*, p. A25.

Dionne, E. J. (2019, May 25). The only bridge Trump is building is to impeachment. *Albuquerque Journal*, p. A14.

Dowd, M. (2016, Oct. 9). Donald goes to the dogs. *The New York Times*, pp. SR1, 3.

Dowd, M. (2019, July 28). Spare me the purity racket. *The New York Times*, p. SR11.

(DSM-5) American Psychiatric Association (2013). *Diagnostic and statistical manual of mental disorders* (5th ed.). Washington, DC: Author.

Fandos, N. (2019). Many dodges, and a few darts, from a tight-lipped witness. *The New York Times*, July 25, 2019, p. A13.

Fingarette, H. (1969). *Self-deception*. London, UK: Routledge & Keegan Paul.

Frances, A. (2017, Feb. 15). An eminent psychiatrist demurs on Trump's mental state. *The New York Times* (letter), p. A26.

Frankfurt, H. G. (2005). *On bullshit*. Princeton, NJ: Princeton University Press.

Friedman, R. A. (2017, Feb. 19). Diagnosing the president. *The New York Times*, p. SR12.

Fromm, E. (2010). *The heart of man: Its genius for good and evil*. Riverdale, NY: American Mental Health Foundation Books. (Original work published in 1964)

Goldberg, M. (2019a). Why aren't we on the road to impeachment? *The New York Times*, April 21, 2019, pp. SR1, 6.

Goldberg, M. (2019b, June 11). Congratulations on fixing the border, Mr. President! *The New York Times*, p. A22.

Gortler, L. & Weininger, S. J. (2010). Chemical relations: William and Lawrence Knox, African American chemists (https://www. sciencehistory.org/distillations/magazine/ chemical-relations-william-and-lawrence-knox-african-american-chemists). *Chemical Heritage Magazine.* Chemical Heritage Foundation. **28** (2).

Grandin, G. (2019, Feb. 21). The insidious myth of the border wall. *The New York Times*, p. A27.

Hayes, C. (2018). What Trump has wrought: Michiko Kakutani examines a drift toward authoritarianism. *The New York Times Book Review*, July 29, p. 12.

Hemingway, E. (2006). *The sun also rises*. New York, NY: Scribner. (Original work published in 1926)

Hitler, A. (2011). *Mein kampf: The official 1939 edition* (J. Murphy, Trans.). Henley in Arden, Great Britain: Coda Books. (Original work published in 1939)

Isaacson, W. (2019, May 12). Richard Holbrooke, the last great freewheeling diplomat [Review of the book *Our man: Richard Holbrooke and the end of the American century*, by G. Packer]. *The New York Times Book Review*, pp. 1, 16, 17.

Jurecic, Q. (2016). On bullshit and the Oath of Office: The "LOL" nothing matters presidency. *Lawfare*, Nov. 23, 2016. https://www.lawfareblog.com/bullshit-and-oath-office-lol-nothing-matters-presidency

Jurecic, Q. (2019, June 8). 3 disturbing episodes from Mueller. *The New York Times*, p. A23.

Kernberg, O. (1970). Factors in the psycho-analytic treatment of narcissistic personalities. *Journal of the American Psychoanalytic Association*, **18**, pp. 51-85.

Kohut, H. (1971). *The analysis of the self: A systematic approach to the psychoanalytic treatment of narcissistic personality disorders.* Chicago, IL: University of Chicago Press.

Lee, B., Ed. (2017). *The dangerous case of Donald Trump: 27 psychiatrists and mental health experts assess a president.* New York, NY: St. Martin's Press.

Lenzenweger, M. F., Clarkin, J. F., Caligor, E., Cain, N. M. & Kernberg, O. F. (2018). Malignant narcissism in relation to clinical change in borderline personality disorder: An exploratory study. *Psychopathology*, **51**: 318-325.

Leonhardt, D. (2019). The people vs. Donald J. Trump. *The New York Times*, Jan. 6, 2019, pp. SR1, 2.

Li, D. K. (2019, Feb. 27). Michael Cohn testimony: The 10 best lines from his hearing before Congress. https://www.nbcnews.com/politics/politics-news/michael-cohen-testimony-10-best-lines-his-hearing-congress-n977116

Lieberman, J. A. (2018, Jan. 15). Maybe he's just a jerk. *The New York Times*, p. A19.

Maccoby, M. (2003). *The productive narcissist: The promise and peril of visionary leadership.* New York, NY: Broadway Books.

Maccoby, M. (2007). *Narcissistic leaders: Who succeeds and who fails.* Boston, MA: Harvard Business School Press.

Malkin, C. (2017). Pathological narcissism and politics: A lethal mix. In B. Lee (Ed.), *The dangerous case of Donald Trump: 27 psychiatrists and mental health experts assess a president* (pp. 54-59). New York, NY: St. Martin's Press.

Masterson, J. F. & Klein, R. (1995). *Disorders of the self: New therapeutic horizons*. New York, NY: Brunner/Mazel.

Mayer, J. (2019). Trump TV: Fox News has always been partisan. But has it become propaganda? *The New Yorker*, March 11, 2019, pp. 40-53.

McHugh, P. R. & Slavney, P. R. (1998). *The perspectives of psychiatry* (2nd ed.). Baltimore, MD: Johns Hopkins University Press.

Morrow, L. (2018, June 23-24). Did an ancient Greek anticipate Trump? *The Wall Street Journal*, p. A13.

Mueller, R. S. (2019a). *The Mueller report*: Presented with related materials by the Washington Post. New York: Scribner.

Mueller, R. S. (2019b). Letting the report speak for itself. *The New York Times*, May 30, 2019, p. A16.

Mr. Mueller's Letter to Mr. Barr (2019). *The New York Times*, May 2, 2019, p. A24.

Muller, R. J. (1987). *The marginal self: An existential inquiry into narcissism*. Atlantic Highlands, NJ: Humanities Press International.

Muller, R. J. (2011). Failing narcissistic defenses can turn love toxic. *The Humanistic Psychologist*, **39**, pp. 375-378.

Muller, R. J. (2014). What kind of narcissist are you? *The Humanistic Psychologist*, **42**, pp. 215-224.

Muller, R. J. (2016, November 15). Can Donald Trump change his spots? *The Baltimore Sun*, p. 11.

Muller, R. J. (2018). *The four domains of mental illness: An alternative to the DSM-5*. New York, NY: Routledge/Taylor & Francis Group.

Ogden, E. (2018, August 5). Donald Trump mesmerist. *The New York Times*, p. SR2.

Ovid (1964). *Ovid's metamorphoses* (R. Humphries, Trans.). Bloomington, IN: Indiana University Press.

Rahn, W. (2019). 10 times Trump may have obstructed justice, according to Mueller. CBS News, July 23, 2019.

Richardson, J. (2014). *Pragmatism and American experience: An introduction*. New York, NY: Cambridge University Press.

Ruiz, R. R. (2019, Feb. 28). Claim puts president at a hush-money scheme's center. *The New York Times*, p. A1.

Sanger, D. E., Wong, E. (2019). "Trump-Kim talks undone by big egos and bad bets." *The New York Times*, March 3, 2019, pp. A1, 10.

Savage, C. (2019a, March 28). Was it obstruction? Investigation closes with an open question. *The New York Times*, p. A18.

Savage, C. (2019b, April 24). Evaluating the clues left on obstruction. *The New York Times*, p. A13.

Schwartz, T. (2017). I wrote *The art of the deal* with Donald Trump: His self-sabotage is rooted in his past. In B. Lee (Ed.), *The dangerous case of Donald Trump: 27 psychiatrists and mental health experts assess a president* (pp. 69-74). New York, NY: St. Martin's Press.

Serota, M. (2019). Donald Trump urges reporters to look at the oranges of the Mueller investigation. April 2, 2019, https://www.spin.com/2019/04/trump-origins-oranges-dad-germany/

Shear, M. D., Fadulu, L. (2019). Trump says hearings gave Republicans a 'good day.' *The New York Times*, July 25, 2019, p. A15.

Stephens, B. (2018, Dec. 22). Dear anonymous inside the Trump administration. *The New York Times*, p. A23.

Trump, D. J., & Schwartz, T. (2015). *Trump: The art of the deal*. New York, NY: Ballantine Books. (Original work published in 1987)

van den Berg, J. H. (1972). *A different existence: Principles of phenomenological psychology*. Pittsburgh, PA: Duquesne University Press.

Williams, P. (2018). Prescient. *The New Yorker*, Nov. 12, pp. 30-31.

Witcover, J. (2019, May 28). Trump's invitation to his own impeachment. *The Baltimore Sun*, p. 11.

Wruble, S. (2017). Trump's daddy issues: A toxic mix for America. In B. Lee (Ed.), *The dangerous case of Donald Trump: 27 psychiatrists and mental health experts assess a president* (pp. 268-280). New York, NY: St. Martin's Press.

Zahavi, D. (2019). *Phenomenology: The basics.* Abingdon, Oxon, UK: Routledge/Taylor & Francis Group.

Appendix A

Can Donald Trump Change His Spots?
The Baltimore Sun, *November 15, 2016*

B y any criterion, Donald Trump is a pathological narcissist. This means that he over-iden-
tifies with a self-created, rigidly held self-image,
which is usually credited to a defense against a
serious psychic insult that occurred early in life.
In the attempt to make his day-to-day experience match that ideal image, Mr. Trump has
become the center of his own world where
everyone else is a mere satellite. His kind of narcissism is considered pathological because his
lack of concern for anyone but himself leads him

to think, feel and act in ways that diminish and damage everyone and everything he touches.

During the campaign, Mr. Trump put on what could be considered a "clinic" of pathological narcissism. From his opinions, he created his own facts. Truth for him is what it needs to be at any given moment. A day later, the need may be different so that what was "true" before takes a 180-degree turn. To some extent, we all create our own worlds, but Mr. Trump does so with little or no regard for the effect his actions will have on others. Only he counts. We have had narcissists at all levels of government before, but none so virulent as this man has shown himself to be.

In February 2015, at the start of his campaign for the presidency, Mr. Trump told a reporter that, as president, he would act differently than he had as a businessman, reality TV mogul and presidential candidate. But how differently?

The gracious Donald Trump we saw and heard on election night was a winner, if unexpectedly. But how would he react if, as president, he lost a major battle with Congress, or was humiliated by a foreign power? Could he authentically handle the kinds of insults to his self-image that would typically require him to make a highly destructive response in the effort to salve his narcissistic wound? Mr. Trump's tenuously held sense of self depends on a constant external reaffirmation of the rigid self-image that is at the core of his being. He withers without attention, particularly media attention. Could he survive the major setbacks that are inevitable in any presidency?

The *Diagnostic and Statistical Manual of Mental Disorders* (DSM-5) considers pathological narcissism a personality disorder, which is defined as "an enduring pattern of inner experience and behavior that deviates markedly from the expectations of the individual's culture." The key word here is "enduring." In the process of a continuous self-creation, pathological narcissists repeat a habitual pattern of thought, emotion and behavior as they interact with others and deal with events they encounter. This pattern, according to the DSM-5, is characterized by grandiosity, need for admiration and lack of empathy. (I should point out that there are healthy iterations of narcissism.)

That said, what we know about the psychobiology of the self tells us that we are psychologically and biologically "plastic," which is to say capable of changing. Pathological narcissism is a deeply entrenched distortion of the self, but one that is always played out with others. The change in environment that Donald Trump will experience when he becomes president in January offers him possibilities for positive change.

Once in the White House, Mr. Trump could discover a higher purpose. This epiphany would require a structural change in his being: a shift from the kind of self-gratification that focuses only on his needs to one that benefits others and the world. So far, everyone and everything in Mr. Trump's life has been about serving and gratifying Donald Trump. But he cannot succeed as president if his behavior continues to be shaped by his narcissistic template. He will not get away with short selling the United States and other nations or reneging on promises he made during the campaign to certain groups (blue collar workers, blacks, Latinos).

We—and Donald Trump—are in uncharted territory. No one knows the limits of what Friedrich Nietzsche called the "will to power," our capacity to use our freedom to accomplish a desired goal. The question is, now that, for the first time, Mr. Trump is explicitly being asked to work for others and not just pursue his own enrichment and gratification, will he rise to the challenge? Even a moderate overcoming, and blunting, of his narcissistic pathology would mean better lives for us all.

Appendix B

How Low Will He Go?

A slightly different version of this text was submitted to The Baltimore Sun *on Feb. 20, 2017 and was rejected.*

Against most of the evidence, some of us held out a sliver of hope that Donald Trump might not be as bad a president as it seemed he could be. Since the first day of his presidency, that vision has steadily dimmed.

Two recent events rise above the noise of this brief administration's previous calamities. On Feb. 13, 2017, Michael Flynn, Trump's national security advisor, was forced to resign after it was revealed that he had lied to Vice President

Michael Spence and the FBI about had having phone conversations with the Russian ambassador to the U.S., Sergey Kislyak, on lifting sanctions that Barack Obama imposed on Russia for hacking Democratic Party officials during the 2016 presidential election.

If it were proven that Trump knew about this forbidden overture, or worse, that he had initiated it, his presidency would have come under heavy fire. If that wasn't enough for one week, three days after Flynn's firing, Trump's first presidential press conference came off as a loopy, 77-minute freak show. *The New York Times* fact checkers identified seven outright lies, involving major issues.

Almost a century ago, in an article for *The Baltimore Sun*, H. L. Mencken, a skeptic about the American version of democracy, let his imagination roam: "On some great and glorious day the plain folks of the land will reach their heart's desire at last, and the White House will be adorned by a downright moron." The majority of those who voted in the 2016 presidential election probably felt that way in the early hours of November 9, as it became clear that Donald Trump would be our next president.

My major worry is that, under the growing pressure of an impossibly conflicted and unimaginably stressful presidency, the malignant narcissist Donald Trump would respond in a way that had far worse consequences for America and the rest of the world than anyone ever anticipated.

Trump, like many who have narcissistic pathology, has sociopathic traits that include habitual lying, defrauding others in business deals and launching into brutal verbal attacks against his reputed enemies. The psychoanalysts Erich Fromm and Otto Kernberg introduced the term "malignant narcissist" to name those whose narcissism is most destructive, and who frequently commit criminal acts, up to and including murder, without remorse. Raymond Reddington, the wily protagonist in NBC's TV series, "The Blacklist," exemplifies this pathology.

If Trump were to be severely tested or humiliated by the leaders of, say, Russia or Iran to a degree that he chose not to tolerate, his potential for aggression and destruction could be unleashed against these countries, in a way everyone would regret. Short of that, I fear Trump will continue to blindly pursue his plan to "make America great again," an idea which, in his hands, lacks any rational meaning or restraint. In the chaos created, many people would undoubtedly suffer. Lacking empathy, Trump would view his victims as soldiers in a battle to put America first, accepting their pain as collateral damage.

It is one thing to throw sand in the gears of some process, which is what Trump has done in his business deals for decades. It is altogether something else to toss in boulders that crush the gears, killing the machine. When threatened with rejection or failure, malignant narcissists try to save themselves by attacking whomever or whatever they feel has not met their expectations. This attempt often destroys both these narcissists and their victims.

Harvard's Abiding Influence on a Career and a Life

I will begin by acknowledging my own narcissism, which has already been partially documented (Muller, 2014), and which, I believe, is mostly productive. My metaphorical "internal mirror" holds many positive, constructive elements that comprise a kind of template for the person I became, and the work I do.

At some point in a life, one needs to take an inventory of the people, institutions and experiences that were the most generative influences. I took such an inventory when it came time to write the acknowledgments section for my seventh book, *The Four Domains of Mental Illness*, in 2018. I came up with 62 names that included parents; other adults, mostly neighbors who contributed significantly to my development in childhood and adolescence; friends; teachers, from high school through graduate school; mentors who worked with me "informally," outside the classroom; and others who influenced me and helped me along the way, in many ways.

Assembling this list, I came to see that it really does "take a village to raise a child"—as the African trope has it—and an adolescent and an adult as well. I have indeed had a munificent village. The occupants ranged from what are generally regarded as ordinary citizens to men who were world-class contributors to their professions.

While mulling the gratitude I felt toward everyone on my "village" list, it dawned on me that five people had been most influential. Specifically—and here my (mostly) productive narcissism becomes evident—they showed me what it meant to hit the highest level of achievement. It is a privilege to record their names and the professions in which they made their reputations: William von Eggers Doering, Lawrence H. Knox and Alex Nickon (organic chemistry); Ralph Harper (existential philosophy); and Paul R. McHugh (Meyerian psychiatry). Each contributed mightily to the person I became and the work I did. All had more significant careers than I have had but working with them helped me to achieve *my* highest level.

Besides brilliance and generosity, these men had one other factor in common: all had spent years at Harvard University, acquiring undergraduate, graduate and professional degrees. The school that nurtured them remotely nurtured me as well. I am eternally grateful to the Harvard of the era that fostered these five luminaries.

During three summers, I worked with William Doering and Lawrence Knox at the Hickrill Chemical Laboratory in Katonah, New York, a short drive from Mt. Kisco, where I was born and raised. Starting after my junior year in high school, I assisted Hickrill's postdocs with their experimental work and was given larger assignments as my skills developed. The lab was underwritten by the Hickrill Chemical Research Foundation, headed by Ruth Alice Norman Weil, who had received a doctorate in chemistry at Columbia under Doering's direction, in 1946.

While director of Hickrill, Bill Doering was Sterling Professor of Chemistry at Yale (he would return to Harvard in 1968 as Mallinckrodt Professor of Chemistry). He spent summers at the lab, living in a small house on the Hickory Hill estate. In this sylvan setting, he was at ease and accessible to me and to Maitland "Mait" Jones Jr., who also worked at the lab, did his PhD with Doering at Yale and went on to have a stellar career at Princeton. From Bill Doering I learned what it means to have ideas that are worth pursuing and how to nurture an idea until it comes to fruition.

Larry Knox, who was assistant director at the Hickrill lab, oversaw Mait Jones and me in our experimental work. His dissertation director at Harvard, the renowned physical organic chemist Paul Doughty Bartlett, said that his work was "the neatest and prettiest job of any research student" there (Gortler & Weininger, 2010). Bill Doering and Mait Jones both credit Larry Knox as being one of the best experimentalists they ever worked with.

Alex Nickon, a protege of Harvard's Louis F. Fieser, played a key role in advising me as I traversed the final stages of my doctoral research at Johns Hopkins, as did his gifted graduate student and later postdoc, my friend Raymond C. Weglein.

I met Ralph Harper and Paul McHugh at Johns Hopkins after finishing formal graduate work there. A student of John Wild at Harvard, Harper was one of a handful of scholars who brought existential philosophy from Europe to the U.S. following World War II. He was also an Episcopal priest and rector of St. James Episcopal Church in Monkton, Maryland. It was a high honor to be taught by him, and to get to know someone who had been a part of the existential revolt against the limitations of analytical and positivistic thinking. This experience proved pivotal in understanding the cause and nature of mental illness, which would eventually become my life's work. Chapter by chapter, Harper carefully critiqued the text of my first book *The Marginal Self: An Existential Inquiry into Narcissism* (Muller, 1987).

Paul McHugh, after 11 years at Harvard, went to the Institute of Psychiatry (now a part of King's College London) to work with Aubrey Lewis, who had been a resident of Adolf Meyer's at Johns Hopkins. At that time, Meyer's influence on psychiatry in the U.S. had been all but obliterated by Freud's psychoanalysis, necessitating McHugh's excursion across the pond to learn Meyerian psychiatry. At Johns Hopkins, McHugh (along with Philip R. Slavney) created the Meyer-informed *Perspectives of Psychiatry*, the inspiration for my *Four Domains of Mental Illness*. McHugh and I talked psychiatry through many hours during the six years I worked on this book. As far as I am concerned, he has the best psychiatric mind in North America.

Though he did not go to Harvard, the light from another life burns in my internal mirror with an intensity equal to that emitted by the five men just mentioned. Edgar Hilliar was organist and choirmaster at St. Mark's Episcopal Church in Mt. Kisco for just over forty years, beginning in 1948. Hilliar was a recognized superstar at the console—E. Power Biggs considered him his top student. How do you make a written text approach the level of the postludes Hilliar played, Sunday after Sunday, and the recitals he gave during all those years? If you are me, you keep retyping and polishing until the computer screen shows text with a "long line," which is always there in the best performances of any music. This inevitable flow of notes, from first to last, carries the listener unobstructed to the end. I have found that a similar linearity and fluidity—a through-line—can be achieved with words in descriptive and analytical writing.

It seems likely that the brilliance, generosity and friendship of these six men affected me through what William James Sr., father of philosopher and psychologist William James and novelist Henry James, described as the "soluble stuff" that one person can absorb by knowing and interacting with another person (Richardson, 2014, p. 83). Inevitably, some of the "soluble stuff" flowing from these giants must have found its way into my internal mirror, and that has made all the difference.

About the Author

René J. Muller is the author, most recently, of *The Four Domains of Mental Illness: An Alternative to the DSM-5*. His previous books include *The Marginal Self* (1987), *Anatomy of a Splitting Borderline* (1994), *Beyond Marginality* (1998), *Psych ER* (2003) and *Doing Psychiatry Wrong* (2008). He is a former Adjunct Assistant Professor of Psychiatry at the University of Maryland School of Medicine and has been a regular contributor to *Psychiatric Times* and a peer reviewer for the annual U.S. Psychiatric and Mental Health Congress. He currently reviews articles for *The Humanistic Psychologist* and for *Philosophy, Psychology, & Psychiatry*. Between 1995 and

2005, he evaluated over 3,000 patients in the emergency room at Union Memorial Hospital and Good Samaritan Hospital, in Baltimore. He holds a PhD from Johns Hopkins University and an MA from Duquesne University. Currently, his main interests are psychiatric diagnosis, psychiatric medicine and identifying the synergy between the compatible and complementary approaches of Meyerian psychobiology and existential psychiatry. A list of all his publications can be found at academia.edu.

He may be contacted at mullerrenej@aol.com.

Made in the USA
Lexington, KY
28 November 2019